THE CROSS
OVER INDIA

THE CROSS
OVER INDIA

by

RAJAIAH D. PAUL

SCM PRESS LTD
56 BLOOMSBURY STREET
LONDON

To the revered memory of
my Father and Mother
to whom I owe more
than words can tell

First published September 1952

Printed in Great Britain by
Northumberland Press Limited
Gateshead on Tyne

CONTENTS

FOREWORD

I learned long since that a bishop who wants a quiet life had better do cheerfully what the laity tell him to do; so when my friend Rajaiah Paul asked me to write a foreword to his book, I agreed without demur.

Most of the books about the Indian Church have been written either by missionaries or by Indian ministers. Mr. Paul is very much a layman, a man who has spent nearly the whole of his life in the service of the government, reaching in that service positions of the highest distinction. But he is also an earnest Christian, who has acquired in his spare time a knowledge of the Bible and of Church History which many ordained ministers might envy. When I add that he is the father of nine extremely human children, and the head of one of the most delightful Christian households in which it has ever been my privilege to stay, I shall have made it plain how well qualified he is to write a layman's book about the Church.

The history of Christianity in India has never been fully or worthily written. It is good therefore that Mr. Paul has reminded us of some stages in that miraculous history, and of some of those forgotten worthies, whose witness has been the life-blood of the growing Church. But I think many readers will find most interesting that part of the book in which Mr. Paul discourses on the present state of the Indian Church and its needs. No missionary would ever have dared to write so frank and damaging a criticism of that Church. Mr. Paul speaks as he writes. Recently at a meeting of the Synod of the Church of South India, he let himself go in some rather tart comments on the spiritual state of the Church and its leadership; the Synod showed a very proper spirit in unanimously re-electing him, against his will, as its General Secretary.

I hope that many readers will ponder the last paragraph of

the book. The evangelisation of India has only been begun, and the need for sincere and humble fellow-workers from the west is felt by all Indian Christians who seriously weigh the present situation. The new missionary could not do better than start by spending a month or two with the Paul family. It would be made plain to him, kindly but quite firmly, exactly where he got off; but he would learn what it is to have Indian Christian friends. Indian Christians do not easily give their confidence or their hearts. But once given, as I know from joyful experience, those precious gifts are never withdrawn.

STEPHEN NEILL

PREFACE

THE distinct purpose of a preface has so far never been defined —except in the dictionary. A preface is sometimes an introduction, sometimes an apology, but most times an advertisement.

'Gentle reader, I presume thou wilt be very inquisitive to know what antick or personate actor this is that so insolently intrudes upon this common theatre to the worlds view, whence he is, why he doth it and what he hath to say.' That is how 'Democritus Junior' addresses himself to the prospective reader of his *Anatomy of Melancholy*. Appropriate enough when Sir Thomas Burton chose to hide himself under a pseudonym.

'It was penned in such a place and with such disadvantage that I had not the assistance of any good book whereby to promote my invention or relieve my memory.' Thus Sir Thomas Browne in his 'To the Reader' in *Religio Medici*.

'It is very seldom that the preface of a book is read; indeed of late years most books have been sent to the world without any. I deem it however advisable to write a preface and to this I humbly call the attention of the courteous reader as its perusal will not a little tend to the proper understanding and appreciation of these volumes.' So wrote George Borrow in his preface to *The Bible in Spain*.

I am afraid I cannot adopt in full any of the above prefatory remarks; but every one of them applies partially to the circumstances under which this book came to be written. The idea was suggested to me by Dr. Hugh Martin when I was in England about two years ago. The S.C.M. Press had long been wanting to get out a book on Christianity in India written by an Indian layman who would have no other purpose in writ-

9

ing it except to say what he feels about it all; and he thought I might be able to produce something which might meet their requirement. I agreed to try my hand at it—and this is the result. This is not a history of Christianity in India. We badly need a complete and up-to-date history of Christianity in India; but it can only be done by a historian and in any case it cannot be done in India. The necessary material is not there but is all in Europe. Nor is this an apologia for Western missionary enterprise. There are several books of that nature and there is no need to add one more. Nor indeed is it a criticism of missionary methods, though a re-examination of them is urgently called for in view of the profound changes that have taken place in recent years in all the mission-fields. This is a meagre, almost cursory, attempt to assess the process and worth of the Christian enterprise in my country in the past and its position at present, with an even slighter attempt to indicate what conditions may be in the near future. It is only in order to give the necessary background to such an assessment that the first five chapters, which are in the main historical, were written. If the book helps anyone to understand a little more of what Christianity in India has achieved and how it did it, the purpose of writing it will have been fully served. In the good providence of God the preaching and the practice of the Christian religion in India are of vital interest to world Christianity; and the Church in India is destined to play in the future an even greater part in the affairs of Christendom than she has done in the past.

That the book is very incomplete and far too condensed will be perceived at the very first glance. One would like to have been able to include many more 'heroes' of the Indian Church, for nowhere else do we see more clearly than in the life-stories of such men how Christianity has affected men's lives and under what handicaps it has had to work in this country. The part which India has played so far and is still likely to play in the Ecumenical movement and in the movements towards Church union needs far more elaboration than has been possible in this small book. A re-examination of missionary methods and of the Christian approach to the other two great religions in this country could not at all be attempted in a book of this size. One wishes that more competent hands than mine would undertake these tasks for the benefit of world Christianity.

The Nilgiris,　　　　　　　　　　RAJAIAH D. PAUL
　　South India
　　　　March 31, 1952.

I

THE BEGINNINGS OF CHRISTIANITY IN INDIA

THERE is not the slightest doubt but that the Indian Church, or at least one portion of it, is historically one of the most ancient Churches in the world; though, for all practical purposes, it must be considered to be one of the 'younger Churches'—to use the phraseology now familiar since Jerusalem 1928 and Tambaram 1938.

Its origins are, however, lost in the mists of antiquity. It is difficult to say whether the claim made by the Syrian Church on the west coast of South India that it was founded by St. Thomas the Apostle is valid. The tradition is that St. Thomas came and preached in India and died a martyr at Mailapore near Madras. As there was considerable trade and cultural intercourse about that time between the Roman Empire and India by sea and by the overland route there is nothing inherently improbable in this tradition.

The story is first told in great detail in the apocryphal *Acts of Apostles*, in which one chapter is devoted to the 'Acts of St. Thomas'. The date of this is most probably the end of the second century. The story itself is well known. St. Thomas while at Jerusalem received a divine command to go to India. He went somewhat unwillingly. King Gondopharus of that country ordered the apostle to build him a magnificent palace and entrusted him with the necessary treasure. The Apostle, instead of busying himself about the construction of the palace, went about preaching the Gospel, healing the sick and distributing the treasures to the poor; and told the king that a

palace had been built for him in heaven. He afterwards
traversed various kingdoms of India, preaching the Gospel
everywhere, till in the territory of a king called Mesdeus, while
he was praying on a hill-top, he was killed by four soldiers
who pierced him through with their lances. Though this
legend cannot be accepted as fully historical, it is difficult to
reject it out of hand. That an Indo-Parthian king by name
Gondopharus ruled over 'India' in the first century, that his
India coincided with the Punjab and Afghanistan, is a fact
proved by the discovery in those regions of several coins bear-
ing his name. And when one remembers that even though
Gondopharus had been mentioned in the apocryphal Acts of
St. Thomas, he was not known to history till his name was
thus discovered on the coins, it is difficult to say that the whole
of that apocryphal book is pure invention. It certainly shows
that very early in the Church it was accepted that St. Thomas
was the Apostle of the Indies. His martyrdom in India is
alluded to and accepted as true in all the ancient martyrologies
and liturgies.

There is, further, the testimony of the Fathers of the
Western Church, beginning from the third century. In the
Paschal Chronicle is a fragment of a work of Bishop Dorotheus
(born 254) in which he relates the acts and journeyings of the
Apostles: 'The Apostle Thomas after having preached the
Gospel to the Parthians, Medes, Persians, Germanians (an agri-
cultural people of Persia mentioned by Herodotus), Bactrians
and Magi, suffered martyrdom at Calamina in India.'

St. Gregory of Nazianzus (born 330, died 390) says in one
of his homilies: 'Were not the apostles strangers amidst the
many nations and countries over which they spread themselves?
What had Paul in common with the gentiles, Luke with
Achaia, Andrew with Epirus, John with Ephesus, Thomas
with India, Mark with Italy?'

St. Ambrose (born 340, died 397) says: 'Even those Kingdoms which were shut out by rugged mountains became access-
ible to them (the apostles) as India to Thomas, Persia to
Matthew.'

St. Jerome (ordained 378, died 420) says : 'He was indeed

at one and the same time with the apostles during the forty days and with the angels and in the Father and in the uttermost ends of the ocean. He dwelt in all places: with Thomas in India, with Peter at Rome, with Titus in Crete, with Andrew in Achaia, with each apostolic man in each and all countries.'

St. Gaudentius, Bishop of Brescia (died between 410-27), in a sermon delivered on the occasion of the dedication of a church named *Basilica Concilii Sanctorum*, 'Assembly of the Saints', at Brescia in 402 (for which church relics of Saints Thomas, John the Baptist, Andrew and Luke had been secured —hence the title) said: 'We possess here the relics of those four who having preached the Kingdom of God and His righteousness were put to death by unbelieving and perverse men and now live for ever in God—John at Sebastena, Thomas among the Indians, Andrew and Luke at the city of Patras.'

St. Paulinus of Nola (born 353, Bishop 409, died 431) says: 'So God, bestowing His holy gifts on all lands, sent His apostles to the great cities of the world. To the Patrians he sent Andrew, to John the charge at Ephesus he gave Europe and Asia, their errors to repel with effulgence of light, Parthia receives Matthew, India Thomas, Libya Thaddeus, and Phrygia Philip.'

To these statements by early Christian writers must be added the testimony of the unvarying tradition of the subsequent centuries. In the sixth century we find Gregory of Tours in his *In Gloria Martyrum,* a work which he revised in 590 shortly before his death, writing: 'St. Thomas the Apostle, according to the narration of his martyrdom, is stated to have suffered in India. His holy remains, after a long interval of time, were removed to the city of Edessa in Syria and there interred. In that part of India where they first rested, stand a monastery and a church of striking dimensions elaborately adorned and designed. . . . This, Theodore, who had been to the place, narrated to us.'

In the Anglo-Saxon Chronicle, under the year 883, there is an entry which says that Sighelm, Bishop of Shereburn, was sent to the tomb of St. Thomas in India by King Alfred the

Great, in fulfilment of a vow. The entry reads: 'The year 883. In this year the army went up the Scheldt to Conde and they sat down one year. And Marinus the Pope then sent *lignum Domini* (a relic of the cross) to King Alfred. And in the same year Sighelm and Aethalstan conveyed to Rome the alms which the King had vowed (to send) thither and also to India to Saint Thomas and Saint Bartholomew, when they sat down against the army at London: and there, God be thanked, their prayer was very successful, after that vow.' This is further supported by William of Malmesbury, who writes (c. 1115): 'Beyond the sea to Rome and to Saint Thomas in India, he (Alfred) sent many gifts. The legate employed for this purpose was Sigelimus, the Bishop of Sherborne, who with great success arrived in India, at which everyone in this age wonders. Returning thence he brought back exotic gems and aromatic liquors which the land there produces.'

It is incredible that such pilgrimages should have been made to countries so distant and at such various epochs if there had not been a general belief in the apostleship of St. Thomas to India, and some place in India which was reputed to be the scene of his martyrdom. 'The body of St. Thomas,' says Marco Polo, who visited Mailapore in 1292, 'lies in the province of Malabar, near an insignificant little town . . . devotion attracts thither a multitude of Christians.'

In the year 1517, certain Portuguese adventurers visited Mailapore, where they saw many ruined buildings, among which was a chapel of mean appearance, and were told by the local residents that St. Thomas was buried in a church of which the only portion remaining was the chapel. They conveyed the information to the Archbishop at Goa; but no action was taken till the year 1522, when Duarte Monezes, Viceroy of Goa, sent a commission to visit Mailapore and search for the body of St. Thomas. They unearthed from beneath the ruins of the ancient church what they believed to be the bones of the apostle. It is said that there was a sepulchre in which, amongst lime and sand, were found some remarkably white bones, the iron point of a lance with part of the wood attached, and a clay vase filled with earth. The coincidence of this discovery with local traditions, and the arrangement of his tomb, left, in the opinion of the Portuguese, no reason to doubt the identity of these remains with those of the apostle. They were, therefore, placed in a silver shrine, and taken to Goa, where they were deposited in a church dedicated to St. Thomas.

Mailapore is about three miles south of Fort St. George. The portion of it near the seashore where the ancient church was situated was renamed by the Portuguese, San Thome. Attached to the Roman Catholic Cathedral in this place is a little chapel, in the floor of which a trap-door gives access to what is popularly regarded as the grave of St. Thomas. Over the altar is a quaint old *Scrinium* with a cruciform reliquary made of brass and set with precious stones, which is said to contain some of the ashes and bones of the apostle, together with fragments of the spear by which he was killed. It must be presumed that these were left behind when the bones of the apostle were taken away to Goa.

In the year 1548, when Jean de Castro was Governor of the Indies, some Portuguese of Mailapore wished to build a chapel upon a hill near the town, said to be the spot where the apostle had been martyred. On beginning the work, they found a stone, with a cross sculptured in relief upon it, two feet long and a foot and a half broad, with the extremities ornamented with open *fleur de lys*, and surmounted by a dove, which appeared to peck the top. Round the cross there was an inscription in strange characters which no one could then read.

This slab of stone is still kept in the chapel on the top of St. Thomas's Mount some eight miles south-west of Fort St. George. The inscription surrounding the cross has since been recognized to be in the ancient Pahlavi language, the language of the Persian empire during the Sassanian dynasty, and may, therefore, date from the seventh or eighth centuries. It makes no reference, however, to St. Thomas.

These two 'holy places' may, therefore, be said to attest the existence of the old tradition, but in no wise to prove it as true. In the face of such persistent and widespread tradition, it is difficult to reject as unworthy of credence the story of the apostleship and martyrdom of St. Thomas in India.

But whatever may be our opinion of this tradition, there is not the slightest reason to doubt that there were Christians in India in the second century of our era. The documentary evidence available for this are the following notices which appear in the writings of Eusebius and Jerome, to the effect that Pantænus, the head of the famous catechetical school at Alexandria, was sent by Demetrius, Bishop of Alexandria, to India at the request of some 'ambassadors' from there.

1. It is said that he (Pantænus) 'displayed such zeal for the divine word that he was appointed as a herald of the Gospel of Christ to the nations of the East and was sent as far as India. . . . It is reported that among persons there who knew Christ, he found the Gospel according to St. Matthew which had anticipated his own arrival. For Bartholomew, one of the apostles, had preached to them and left with them the writing of Matthew in the Hebrew language which they had preserved till that time.' (Eusebius: *Ecclesiastical History*, Bk. V, Ch. 10.)

2. 'Pantænus, a philosopher of the Stoic school, according to some old Alexandrian custom, where from the time of Mark the evangelist the ecclesiastics were always doctors, was of so great prudence and erudition both in scripture and secular literature that on the request of the legates of the nation, he was sent to India by Demetrius, Bishop of Alexandria, where he found that Bartholomew, one of the twelve apostles, had preached the advent of the Lord Jesus, according to the Gospel of Matthew, and on his return to Alexandria, he brought this with him in Hebrew characters.' (Jerome: *Liber de Viris Illustribus*, Ch. XXXVI.)

3. 'Pantænus, a philosopher of the Stoic school, was on account of his great reputation for learning sent by Demetrius, Bishop of Alexandria, to India to preach Christ to the Brahmans and philosophers there.' (Jerome: *Epistola LXX ad Magnum oratorem urbis Romae.*)

There is no reason to doubt that the country visited by the learned Pantænus was India, because nowhere else do we find

Brahmins. He laboured there for only a short time, returned to Alexandria and resumed charge of the school from Clement, who, in a well-known passage, speaks of Indian Gymnosophists and 'other barbarian philosophers'. 'Of these,' he says, 'there are two classes, some of them called Sarmanae and others Brahmans; and those of the Sarmanae, who are called Hylobii, neither inhabit cities, nor have roofs over them, but are clothed in the bark of trees, feed on nuts, and drink water in their hands. . . . They know not marriage or begetting of children.' Clement is here clearly referring to the wandering *sadhus* of India, and no doubt got all his information about India from his *guru* Pantænus.

The next record we have of the existence of a Church in India is that at the Council of Nicaea (A.D. 239) a prelate of the ? Indian Church was present and subscribed as 'Metropolitan of Persia and of the Great India'. We then read of the visit to India of two brothers, Frumentius and Edesius, thirty years later. Frumentius obtained the good will of the king of the country, rose high in his favour and helped him in his administration. Discovering among the subjects certain who were Christians, he helped them to build churches and propagate the Gospel. Returning to Alexandria and relating the whole story to Bishop Athanasius, who had by then been elevated to that see, he entreated him to send a Bishop to India. The prelate asked Frumentius to take upon himself the Bishopric. He accepted and returned to India in the year 356 as Bishop of that country. Rufinus, an Italian who had spent twenty-six years in a monastery in Palestine, where he had become intimate with Jerome, returned to Italy in 397, wrote an Ecclesiastical History and died in 412. It is he who gives us this interesting narrative (Rufinus: *Hist. Eccles. Lib.* i, *Cap.* 9).

The first undisputed testimony to the existence of a Church in South India is, however, that of Cosmos, a merchant of Alexandria who was surnamed Indicopleustes (i.e., the Indian voyager), who visited India in the sixth century and who, after spending several years trading with the country, retired into a cloister and wrote several works. He says in one of them:

' In the Malabar country also, where pepper grows, there are Christians, and in Calliana as they call it there is a bishop who comes from Persia where he was consecrated.'

In the ninth century, during the reign of Ceram Perumal, Rajah of Malabar, a wealthy Armenian merchant named Thomas Cana came with a large party and settled in the country. By their diligence and success they brought themselves under the favourable notice of the Rajah. Thomas Cana used his influence to obtain for the Christians in those parts certain immunities and privileges which were embodied, as was the practice in those days, on certain copperplate documents engraved in the old Malayalam script which were long in the possession of the Syrian Christians.

In A.D. 920, the Church was visited by Mar Sapores and Mar Pheroz, two Syrian ecclesiastics from Babylon, who stayed in the country for several years and successfully propagated their religion.

We know nothing about the condition of the Christians of Malabar during the next six hundred years. The period between the death of Ceram Perumal and the coming of the Portuguese about the end of the fifteenth century is a blank. With the coming of the Portuguese a new chapter begins both for the Syrian Church and for the country.

II

THE ROMAN CHURCH COMES
WITH THE PORTUGUESE

CHRISTIAN intercourse between India and Europe, which had begun as early as the second century and had been maintained right down to the tenth, was completely cut off when Mohammedanism became rampant in the Middle East. After the collapse of the Nestorian Church in Persia, and the conquest of India itself by the Mongols, the Church in India became entirely isolated. It dwindled in numbers and, sheltering itself behind the mountains of Travancore and Cochin, escaped severe persecution and just managed to keep itself alive.

For over seven centuries the Arabs successfully prevented all contact between the East and the West, both commercial and religious. It was not till the traders of Arabia yielded the commerce of the Indian seas to the merchants of Genoa and Venice that intercourse was resumed. The travels of Marco Polo in India and China excited the curiosity as well as the cupidity of the people of Europe; and the merchants of Europe, who had hitherto known no other sea-route than those through the Red Sea and the Persian Gulf, now set about to discover another channel through which to import into Europe the wealth of the oriental marts. Towards the close of the fifteenth century, for the first time, the great experiment of a western passage to India round the southernmost tip of Africa succeeded; and on May the 22nd, 1498, Vasco da Gama, a Portuguese adventurer, reached Calicut on the south-western coast of India. This dates a new epoch in the history of the Christian Church in India. The Portuguese followed up this discovery with such assiduity that within the next twenty-five years they had acquired several ports in India and had well entrenched themselves in the country. For a century they carried on their trade without a rival and gradually established complete dominion over quite a large part of the country.

When the Portuguese landed in Malabar they were surprised to see a flourishing Christian community there by whom they were eagerly welcomed as fellow-religionists. They were, however, chagrined to find that though these Christians belonged to a regularly constituted Church with deacons, priests (or *Catanars*) and Bishop (or *Metran*) who came from Mosul in Mesopotamia, then the seat of the ancient Patriarchate of Persia, they knew nothing about the Pope of Rome and owed no allegiance to the Roman Church.

A second expedition was undertaken by the Portuguese soon after the return of Vasco da Gama. This was under the command of Don Pedro Alvares de Cabral and reached Cranganore on the west coast of India in the year 1500. It was Cabral who brought to Europe the first intelligence of the Christian Churches in Malabar. Having made the acquaintance of several Christians of the neighbourhood, he persuaded two of them, brothers, by name Matthias and Joseph, to sail back with him to Europe. The elder of the two, Matthias, died at Lisbon soon after arrival there. Joseph visited Rome and Venice, in which latter place he published, in Latin, an account of himself and of the Church to which he belonged, under the title of *The Travels of Joseph the Indian*; and later apparently succeeded in getting back to India.

In February 1502 Vasco da Gama, with the title 'Admiral of the Indian, Persian and Arabian seas', came to India a second time and anchored in the harbour of Cochin. Whilst he was bartering goods with the people of the country and negotiating with the Rajah for trade privileges, he was visited by a deputation of local Christians who presented him with a petition praying him to take them under his protection and that of his Christian master, expecting thereby to enjoy greater advantages and freedom from the petty tyranny which they were undergoing at the hands of the Hindu King and the powerful Moslem traders who had then the monopoly of the coastal trade. As a token of their submission to the King of Portugal, they sent His Majesty a rod of vermilion wood tipped at both ends with silver, with three little bells at its head, said to be the sceptre of their Christian kings. As a further proof of the confidence reposed in the Portuguese, their Bishop also handed over for safe custody to the commissary of Cochin the six plates of copper on which their ancient rights and privileges were recorded.

This began a terrible chapter in the history of the Church in India. These first European settlers in India were the most un-Christian of men, intent only upon worldly conquest and the acquisition of easy wealth. They lived most immoral lives. They were, no doubt, accompanied by Franciscan friars, but these troubled themselves little about the propagation of Christianity. To the Portuguese Viceroy spreading the Gospel was not a Christian obligation but a matter of state policy. He was anxious to proselytize and get a large number under nominal allegiance to the Church in order to strengthen Portuguese power. Albuquerque, we are told, 'in order to breed up soldiers, very wisely got the Indian maids made Christians and married them to the Portuguese that they might not always stand in need of fresh supplies of men from Portugal'.

Things, however, became a little different when, in the year 1540, under the leadership of Ignatius Loyola, a new spiritual movement was set afoot and the 'Clerks Regular of the Society of Jesus'—the most powerful missionary organization the world has yet seen—inaugurated under a Papal Edict. One of the first acts of Loyola was to send out as a missionary to the East his friend and follower, Francis Xavier. The arrival, on May 6th, 1542, of Francis Xavier at Goa, which had become the capital of the Eastern empire of Portugal, marked the beginning of the missionary activities of that order which were to bear such noble and lasting fruit. Francis Xavier went up and down that long coast on foot, with a bell in his hand, inviting people to gather round him to hear the first rudiments of the Christian truth. He lived in India, however, for only three years; but they were years of incessant activity and arduous labour. His superhuman energies seem to have been attended with almost miraculous results and in the short time he spent in the villages of the south-west coast of India he is said to have converted 700,000 unbelievers to the Christian faith. He literally wore himself out in the service of the Gospel, and while on a voyage to China, where he had planned a similar crusade, died on the 2nd of December, 1552.

His successors, however, who did not have his ardent passion for souls nor his zeal for his Master, directed their energies mainly towards undermining the Malabar churches, which they had decided to bring under the domination of Rome. An inquisition was set up in Goa and the whole Syrian Church declared heretical. Alternately using methods of cajolery and coercion, the Roman Catholic hierarchy tried their best for a whole century to bring the Syrian Church under the domination of Rome. They imprisoned several of the Syrian prelates till there came a time when the Syrian Church was without a Bishop. Things became worse when Don Alexis de Menezes was appointed Archbishop of Goa. He went down to the south with an imposing military force and summoned the Syrian Churches to submit themselves to his authority. The Churches were then under an Archdeacon who, while fully sensible of the impending danger, was so terrorized that he subscribed to a document by which all persons acknowledging any other supremacy than that of the Roman Pontiff were excommunicated. But the people demurred and tried, by a desperate effort, to sweep the Portuguese intruders from their shores. Menezes, however, was too clever and too pitiless a tyrant to allow himself to be worsted in such a conflict. He substituted fraud for violence, while money took the place of arms. He bribed those whom he could not bully and deceived one after another of the leaders; and finally, when he found that the strength of the Syrian Christians was too great for him, he called in the aid of the native Princes. Having obtained the help of the Hindu Rajah of Cochin, he summoned a synod at a place called Udiamperur (Europeanized into and better known as Diamper) on the 20th of June, 1599. The objects of the synod were explicitly stated to be 'for the increase and exaltation of the Catholic faith among the Syrians in Malabar; for the destruction of the errors and heresies which had been sown in the diocese by several heretics and schismatics; for the purging of books from the false doctrines contained in them; for the perfect union of this Church with the whole Church Catholic and universal; for the yielding of obedience to the supreme Bishop of Rome, the Universal pastor of the Church and successor in the chair of St. Peter, and vicar of Christ upon earth, from whom they had for some time departed; for the extirpation of simony, which had been practised in the diocese; for the regulating of the administration of the holy sacraments of the Church, and the necessary use of them; and for the reformation of the affairs of the Church and the clergy, and customs of all the Christian people of the diocese.'

A confession of faith was proclaimed at the synod which the Archdeacon and all the priests were compelled to accept. The Syrian priests, finding no way of escape, repeated the confession and thus bowed their necks to the yoke of Rome. The constitution of their Church was materially altered by the decrees of this synod and they were obliged to acknowledge the supremacy of the Pope. The decrees, involving belief in transubstantiation and purgatory, adoration of the Blessed Virgin, acceptance of the seven sacraments, adoption of the use of images and celibacy of the clergy—articles till then foreign to the Syrian Church—were declared binding: and all those who did not obey were branded as heretics and subjected to the Inquisition which had been set up in Goa. It was, however, with sullen submission that the Syrian clergy yielded. The laymen continued to be vehement in their protests, and persistent in their refusal to accept these strange dogmas.

The Archbishop followed up the proceedings of the synod with violent measures, and grievously persecuted the Syrian Church. He separated priests from their wives, excommunicated, on trifling grounds, members of the Churches; and, with incredible barbarism, destroyed all the old Syriac records which contained proofs of the purity of their faith. His policy seemed to succeed. For sixty years the ascendancy of Rome was maintained, although the Syrian Christians never ceased to make attempts to restore their connection with the Eastern Church. A Bishop by name Ahatulla (i.e., Theodore) was sent to them at their earnest request from Antioch; but he was, on arrival, taken prisoner by the Portuguese, carried to Goa, handed over to the Inquisition and burnt alive as a heretic in 1654. By an interposition of Divine Providence, the decline of the Portuguese power in India commenced at the very period when the chains of submission to Rome had become most galling.

While the official hierarchy was thus pursuing its nefarious policy of subjugating an independent Church, Jesuit missionaries, who were more true to their calling than these Portuguese ecclesiastics, were doing missionary work in other places in the Southern Peninsula. At the commencement of the seventeenth century, Robert de Nobilibus, a nephew of Cardinal Bellarmine and a near relative of Pope Marcellus II, laid the foundations of the Madura Mission. Rejecting the example of Xavier, whose warm heart had expanded towards the poor and oppressed, Robert de Nobilibus, his associates and successors, addressed themselves to the dominant class and sought their converts among the Brahmins. They studied the vernacular and made themselves familiar with the thoughts and customs of the people, and, calling themselves Western Brahmins, they adopted Indian dress, followed Indian customs and even some Hindu religious ceremonies after slight adaptation. They went about clothed in saffron cloth, with marks of sandal-wood on their foreheads, grew their hair long in Indian fashion, carried copper vessels in their hands, and wore wooden sandals. They ate no animal food and performed their ablutions in the manner of the Brahmins. They performed marriages between children, observing all the Hindu ceremonies, and encouraged the performance of the funeral obsequies prescribed by that religion. They did not attempt to break down caste, which is the greatest obstacle to the spread of the Gospel in India. They allowed high- and low-caste Christians to worship apart. These methods gained for them temporary popularity: but the Brahmins soon saw through the trickery and drove them out of Madura. The Christianity of Madura under the Jesuits was a shameful parody of the Christian faith. The result was that they soon lost all their influence. As the Abbé Dubois says in his letters, 'The Hindoos soon found that those missionaries whom their colour, their talents, and other qualities had induced them to regard as extraordinary beings, as men coming from another world, were in fact nothing else but disguised *Fringy* (Europeans); and their country, their religion and original education, were the same with those of the vile, the contemptible *Fringy*, who had of late invaded their country . . . Christianity became more and more an object of contempt and aversion in proportion as the European manners became better known to the Hindoos.'

Soon, the Dutch appeared on the southern coast and established strongholds in Nagapatam, Quilon and Cranganore. They neglected the churches and devoted themselves entirely to commercial pursuits. But, although they showed no particular interest in the Syrians, yet they rendered them useful service by ordering all Romish ecclesiastics to quit the country. The suppression of the Jesuit order in Europe by order of Pope Clement in the year 1773 put an end to their activities and they disappeared from the Indian coasts for a time.

The Syrian Church was thus once more free, and in 1665 a Bishop named Mar Gregorios, who had been consecrated by the Jacobite Patriarch of Antioch, arrived safely in the country and was enthusiastically welcomed everywhere as a liberator from spiritual tyranny. During the three hundred years that have since elapsed, the Syrian Church or at least a portion of it has maintained its connection with the Jacobite Patriarch who resides at Mardin in Armenia. (The term Jacobite is derived from Jacobus Baradeus who adopted the tenets of the Eutychians in the sixth century.) There were, however, others who continued to be part of the Roman Church, but using the Syriac tongue instead of Latin.

During the hundred and thirty years of Dutch occupation, they took little or no interest in the well-being of the Syrian

Church or in the propagation of the Gospel. The English succeeded the Dutch in 1795, and soon instituted an enquiry into the condition of the Christian population of Malabar. For this purpose, Dr. Claudius Buchanan, a chaplain in West Bengal, was commissioned by Lord Wellesley to visit the Syrian Church in 1806. In this work he obtained the cordial assistance of Colonel Macaulay, the first British Resident in Travancore. *The Christian Researches*, published soon after this visit, excited the liveliest interest among Christians in England. One practical result that followed was that the Church Missionary Society undertook a mission to the Syrian Church in the year 1816-17 at the invitation of Colonel Munro, the Resident who succeeded Colonel Macaulay. Messrs. Bailey, Baker, Fenn and Norton were the first missionaries. The object of the mission was to aid the Syrian Church to reform itself without in any way interfering with its liberties. A college was established at Cottayam for the better education of Syrian youth intended for the ministry. For twenty years, this connection with the Syrian Church was maintained happily, but later it had to be severed and the mission withdrawn.

Internal dissensions in the Church followed. One Mar Athanasius Matthew, who had been educated in the college at Cottayam and later at the Church Missionary Society's theological institution in Madras, went to Mardin in Armenia and was ordained first as deacon, thereafter as *cattanar* (priest), subsequently as *ramban* or archdeacon, and finally as Metropolitan in 1842. He came back to Malabar in 1843 to take possession of his see. Then difficulties began. Mar Cheppat Dionysius who had by a royal proclamation been declared Bishop of the Syrians refused to vacate the see. Representations were made to the Patriarch who sent one Mar Koorilas (Cyril) to make enquiries on the spot. On his arrival in Malabar, he promptly declared himself Metropolitan of Malankarai, forging certain papers in order to support his claim. An appeal was then made to the Resident and the Dewan of Travancore. After due enquiry, the claims of Mar Koorilas were found to be spurious: and Mar Athanasius was declared Metropolitan by royal proclamation. This was in 1852. In

1868, Mar Athanasius Matthew consecrated his cousin Thomas as his successor and died in July 1877. This led to disputes regarding succession, and for ten years unseemly litigation went on in the law courts. The evil effects of these dissensions have, however, since been partially remedied.

The Syrian Christian community is now one of the leading Christian communities in India, economically and intellectually well advanced and exhibiting a remarkable spirit of progress and adventure. Religiously, they are still divided. Apart from those who still form part of the Roman Church, there is the Jacobite or Orthodox section owning allegiance to the Patriarch of Antioch. There is also the Mar Thoma Syrian Church which came into existence when a number of Syrians, anxious to reform themselves, but unwilling to be drawn into the Anglican fold, formed themselves into a new section. These have since been the leaders in missionary, social and educational work, and have produced some outstanding figures both in public and in church life.

III

THE COMING OF PROTESTANT
CHRISTIANITY TO INDIA

T H E ninth of July deserves to be perpetually commemorated
in the Indian Church as the date which marked the beginning,
in the year 1706, of what is perhaps the greatest missionary
enterprise since the Apostolic age. On that day there landed
on the shores of India the first two of a long line of intrepid
adventurers for God who within a period of two hundred
and fifty years have succeeded in creating a new and vigorous
Church, nine million strong, in an ancient land with a religious
culture which is like no other in the world. To Denmark,
and more especially to its Christian King, Frederick IV, belongs the honour of inaugurating this glorious missionary
movement which has profoundly affected the life of a great
country and has shaken to its very foundations its age-long
religious and social systems.

The beginning of the first Protestant mission to India is
another instance of religion following in the wake of commerce and political conquest. The success of the Portuguese
in India attracted the attention and stimulated the adventurous
spirit of other European nations. Dutch, Danes, English and
French all came to India and tried to establish not merely trade
connections, but also colonial empires. It was during the reign
of King Christian IV that the Danes first cast their eyes towards the East Indies. An East India Company was established
in the year 1616 and the first Danish trade expedition to India
was sent in 1620 under the command of Ove Gedde, who
negotiated with the Rajah of Tanjore and purchased from him

Tranquebar and a small territory round about for a Danish settlement. Tarangambadi, 'the village of the lapping wavelets' (Europeanized into Tranquebar), was destined to become famous throughout Christendom, not only as the cradle of the earliest Protestant mission to India, but also as the birthplace, two hundred years later, of a movement towards unity in the Church which was among God's plans for it. Though now shorn of its glory as a centre of trade, it has always been looked upon with affection and natural reverence in the Indian Church. When James Lynch, the first Methodist missionary to India, landed in 1816 he made a pilgrimage to Tranquebar, and there at the graves of the first pioneers pledged himself to the service of India and drew the necessary inspiration for his work. This was ultimately to result in the formation of an extensive province of the Methodist Church which is now making a magnificent contribution to the life of the new Church of South India. It was in Tranquebar, too, that Ringeltaube and his immediate successors prepared themselves, spiritually and linguistically, for their service under the London Missionary Society in Travancore, before they proceeded to their field of work.

It was the pious Danish King, King Frederick IV, who, in consultation with Prof. Franck of Halle University, arranged to send two young men, Heinrich Plutchau and Bartholomaus Ziegenbalg, 'who feared God from their hearts and were willing to go to the heathen'; and who had been trained especially for their work by the learned and missionary-hearted professor, as the first missionaries to India. Leaving Copenhagen on the 29th of November 1705, they reached Tranquebar on the 9th of July 1706, after a long and tedious voyage, which, however, gave them time to plan the methods of work which they proposed to adopt in their great and un-precedented task. In the instructions which he gave Ziegenbalg, the good king said, 'Having by the grace of God safely arrived in the country he shall, in the name of Jesus, heartily calling upon the same, at once begin the work for which he is sent out; and shall labour among the pagans as existing circumstances shall make it practicable. He shall always specially betake himself to God's word not doubting that God will make the power laid therein to prove effectual among the heathens. He has to instruct the ignorant in the first principles of the Christian doctrine with all possible simplicity so that the needful foundation may be laid the earlier. In order that the poor blind heathens may understand that the missionary himself has in his heart what he teaches, he must always show himself a pattern of good works, so that also by this his conduct they may be won over. He shall not forget daily to pray for the co-operating grace of God.'

At first, the missionaries received neither sympathy nor co-operation from the Danish officials, who looked upon their venture as something wholly unnecessary and hopelessly impossible of success, and likely to inconvenience the smooth progress of their commerce. In spite of the ministrations of their chaplain, religion was at a very low ebb among the Europeans, who united to oppose the missionaries in every way possible. But 'disowning discouragement' and refusing to be diverted from the sole purpose of their coming, the missionaries set about their work, completely relying upon God, and not on man, to prosper it. 'As we had no human friend or counsellor,' they say, 'of whom we could ask advice, we laid every one of our perplexities before our Father in Heaven, and He never failed to help us.' They began, as is very natural and absolutely necessary, diligently to learn Tamil, the language of the people of the place, and soon became proficient in its use. Tamil is a very ancient Indian language with a voluminous classical literature of very high merit; but it is a complicated one for foreigners to learn, having no less than two hundred and eighteen characters in its alphabet and a very extensive vocabulary. At that time there was no grammar, dictionary or reading book which foreigners could use. So they put themselves to school with a native teacher, and day by day sat with the children repeating every lesson and writing the letters with their fingers on the sand. In spite of the difficulty in getting access to the sacred literature of the Hindoos which were all inscribed on palmyra leaves and zealously kept away from the sight and touch of all foreigners, they succeeded in acquiring a profound knowledge of the religious system which they had come to overthrow. So wide and deep was their knowledge of Hindu religion and theology that the Brahmins (the hereditary priestly class) became alarmed and succeeded in terrorizing and hounding away from Tranquebar their first *munshee* (vernacular teacher) who had taught them for two years.

No sooner had the missionaries acquired a sufficient knowledge of the local vernacular to make themselves intelligible, than they gathered the people, both adult and children, and taught them the basic truths of Christianity, besides engaging themselves in religious discussions with the leading Brahmins and Mohammedans.

The first results of their work were seen in the baptism, on the 12th of May 1707, within ten months after their arrival, of five of the Portuguese slaves, in Zion Church, the European church in the fort. These were literally the slaves of the Danish and German Europeans of the place, having sold themselves to their European masters in exchange for cash, food and raiment. Zion Church being exclusively reserved for the use of Europeans, the missionaries soon set about erecting a separate church as the centre of their missionary activities and spent on it all that they could spare from their own meagre salaries. It was completed in two months and was consecrated, on the 15th of August 1707, 'in the presence of a great conflux of heathens, Mohammedans and Christians who had a sermon preached to them both in Portuguese and in Malabarik', and received the name 'Jerusalem'. On the 5th of September, they baptized nine adult Tamilians, the first fruits of their labour among the Hindus. Several more were baptized on the 15th.

The continual opposition of the European residents of the place came to an end when in July 1709 three more missionaries arrived, bringing with them a considerable sum of money and a letter from their royal patron who sent out positive commands to the Governor of Tranquebar to assist the missionaries to the utmost of his power. The dissolute lives of the European laity, however, continued to be a great stumbling block.

B

It was also in the year 1709 that the people of England came
to know of the work of these missionaries, when some of their
letters to a friend in Germany were translated into English and
published in London. The interest of the Society for Promoting Christian Knowledge (which had been formed in 1698)
was immediately aroused. Subscriptions were invited in support of the mission and there was such a favourable response
that the Society was able to have the Portuguese translation of
the New Testament (made by J. F. d'Almeida, a Roman
Catholic priest who had joined the Evangelical Church in
Batavia) reprinted at Amsterdam and to send many hundred
bound copies to the missionaries at Tranquebar together with
a present of money. A brief notice of the mission was in-
cluded in the Society's report for that year. From then onwards
the S.P.C.K. continued to help the work, till at last, when aid
from Germany and Denmark altogether ceased, it took over
the work completely.

The next task which the missionaries undertook was the
translation of the New Testament into Tamil—fully realizing
that if only the word of God could be placed in the hands of
the people in their own language, it would do its own mighty
work of redemption. Never before had the Bible been translated into an Indian language, and the difficulties of producing
an adequate translation were immense. But Ziegenbalg made
himself responsible for it. He began it in 1708, and by March
1711 he was able to say, 'All the books of the New Testament
are now translated; this is a treasure in India, which surpasses
all other treasures.' Having heard how much money had to be
spent and how much trouble was involved in the copying of
books, the S.P.C.K. decided to despatch a printing press with
Roman letters and all necessary apparatus. It found and trained
one James Fincke and, having obtained a free passage from the
East India Company both for press and printer, they despatched
both in 1711. Fincke died during the voyage, but the press
arrived in India in August 1712. The missionaries for-
tunately discovered among the Company's soldiers one who
understood printing, and they began at once to print cate-
chisms, hymn books, etc., in Portuguese. Later, a fount

of Tamil characters was received from Germany and the missionaries themselves succeeded in casting similar types and in manufacturing the necessary paper. The first printed copies of the New Testament in Tamil were issued from the press in the year 1714. By that time nearly three hundred converts had been made; and the schools started by the missionaries contained upward of eighty children.

In the year 1711 Plutchau went home owing to ill-health and did not return. Ziegenbalg followed in 1714 and was absent from the country for nearly two years. He visited Germany, Denmark and England, and was received everywhere with great cordiality. The Society had then a chance to get first-hand information about the work in which it was helping. He was received in special assembly by the Society and mutual congratulations were exchanged. As soon as Ziegenbalg returned to Tranquebar he found that the church built in 1707 had become too small for the growing congregation and set about erecting a second, bigger one. The foundation stone was laid on the 9th of February 1717, and it was consecrated on the 11th of October 1717, under the name of New Jerusalem Church.

During the last few months of 1718, however, Ziegenbalg's health became indifferent, but he refused to relax or take rest. He steadily grew worse, and died on the 23rd of February 1719, after having handed over the superintendence of the mission to Grundler earlier in the month. He had spent only about ten years in the country, but the arduous work, together with the rigours of the unaccustomed climate, had taken their toll and he died when only thirty-six years of age—the first of the missionary martyrs from the west to India. He was buried in the New Jerusalem Church on the right side of the altar where a tablet in brass still marks his grave.

On the 1st of January 1719 the Archbishop of Canterbury wrote a very encouraging letter to Ziegenbalg, but it arrived after his death. The Archbishop said, ' I consider that your lot is far higher than all Church dignitaries. Let others be prelates, patriarchs, and popes; let them be adorned with purple and scarlet; let them desire bowings and genuflections;

you have won a greater honour than all these. And when that day comes when the great Shepherd shall reward his sheep each one according to his work, a far more magnificent recompense will be given to you, for you shall be taken in the holy company of the Prophets, Evangelists, and Apostles; and shall with them shine like suns among the stars for ever. So wishes and prays, venerable man, your faithful fellow-labourer in Christ, William Cantuar.'

Grundler carried on the work single-handed till in September 1719 three colleagues arrived—Benjamin Schultze, Nikolaus Dahl and J. Heinrich Kistenmacher. They had been sent out in a hurry without ordination. Grundler, apparently knowing that his own end was near, ordained Schultze in February 1720. He himself died on the 19th March 1720, aged 43 years, and was buried on the left side of the altar in New Jerusalem Church.

Schultze faithfully carried on the work. He translated several hymns and published in 1723 a *Hymnologia Tamulica* containing a hundred and twelve hymns. He also continued and completed Ziegenbalg's translation of the Old Testament which he had left at the book of Ruth, and published it in 1725. The conversion in February 1727 of one Wedappan, a Hindu priest-magician, a potter by caste, who used to go about from village to village in wooden sandals set with sharp spikes, passing for a devotee of the goddess Mariamma and collecting alms, caused a great sensation and was an indication of the progress the new faith was making. He had already acquired some Tamil books published by the Tranquebar missionaries, had read them diligently and intelligently, and had to a certain extent been affected by what he had read. He met Schultze on a visit to his village on the 26th of April 1725, and had a long conversation with him. After that, the missionaries visited him often, till in December 1726 he came with his father and three children to beg for baptism. The Brahmins began to persecute him, whereupon he took refuge in one of the Company's villages near Tranquebar. He was instructed further in the faith and was baptized on the 2nd of February 1727.

Three new missionaries, Bosse, Pressier and Walther, arrived on the 19th of June 1725, giving great relief to Schultze. At the suggestion of the S.P.C.K., he began to think of a mission to the people in the British dominions. The necessary leave was obtained from the East India Company; and Schultze went to Madras in 1726 (walking all the way) and founded a new mission there, with Sartorius as his assistant. Schultze was to receive £60 a year and Sartorius £45. The charges for a catechist, a schoolmaster, one servant, the rent of a house and the support of children in school were also paid by the Society. Gifts of 'books, paper, binding tools, knives, medicines, toys for children, looking-glasses, studs, sleeve buttons, ivory combs, blue necklaces, glass' were also sent to him. There is even mention in the invoices of 'a Cheshire Cheese, Three chests cont. 3 Gross Beer and Half a chest of wine'.

Here Schultze found it necessary to learn Telugu (another language spoken by a large number of the people in and to the north of Madras), translated the short catechism and later the New and Old Testaments into that language, and published them between 1727 and 1732. By 1730 he had collected a congregation of more than two hundred. In 1737 he began to study and do translations in Hindustani, the language of the Mohammedans of the south of India. Unfortunately, he found it difficult to agree with his colleagues, as he was of a somewhat dictatorial character and senior to them. He remained in Madras till 1743 when, after twenty-four years in India, he returned to Europe broken in health, leaving the Madras Mission in the charge of Johann Philipp Fabricius. The Christians baptized by him in Madras amounted to seven hundred. He recovered his health in Europe and lived for several years in Halle, still serving the missionary cause by the publication of literature and the instruction of students. Among the youths who listened to his Indian experiences was Christian Frederic Schwartz who was later to become one of the Church's greatest missionary heroes.

Work in Tranquebar was also progressing satisfactorily. The need for ordaining suitable Indian candidates for the priesthood soon became apparent. Scattered congregations in

the villages round about needed constant attention if they were
to grow in spirituality, and the missionaries found it impossible
to visit them as frequently as was necessary. They therefore
wrote to the Mission College at Copenhagen asking for instructions; and received authority to carry out their good
intention. The missionaries, however, waited for nearly five
years, and then, after elaborate and careful preparation,
ordained Aaron on the 28th of December 1733 as a priest—a
step which, though taken so hesitantly, was fully justified by
the sequel.

It was in July 1750 that the eminent missionary, Christian
Frederic Schwartz, a veritable hero of the cross and a star of
the first magnitude among the wonderful galaxy of missionaries of the eighteenth century, began his labours. His outstanding abilities and extraordinary talents soon became
apparent. He preached his first Tamil sermon within four
months of his arrival. He could minister to the Portuguese,
as he was proficient in their language also. In 1753 the
brethren at Tranquebar gave him the superintendence of all
the work south of the River Cauveri. When the jubilee of the
Tranquebar mission was celebrated on the 9th of July 1756, it
was found that there were eleven thousand persons who had
embraced the gospel of Christ during fifty years.

The dislocation caused by the war then raging in the Car-
natic did not seriously affect the work, chiefly because Tranquebar was a Danish settlement. The missionaries visited new
regions and set up stations in various other places. In 1758
Schwartz visited Negapatam, and in 1760 Jaffna, Colombo
and Point de Galle in the Island of Ceylon, spending
several months there preaching to both Christians and
heathens.

In 1761, accompanied by Kohlhoff, he undertook a missionary
tour to Cuddalore and Madras, and in the following year went
on foot to Tanjore and to Trichinopoly, where there was a military garrison, a school-room, and later a spacious church, built
with the help of the Commandant, Col. Wood, and opened
on the 18th of May 1766. When the S.P.C.K. decided to establish a mission in Trichinopoly, Schwartz was chosen to found

it, being willingly spared for this by his fellow missionaries at Tranquebar. In 1767 he settled down at Trichinopoly and became one of the regular missionaries. 'Here on an income of forty-eight pounds a year, dressed in dimity dyed black, eating rice and vegetables cooked in native fashion and living in a room of an old building just large enough to hold himself and his bed, Schwartz devoted himself to his apostolic duties among the inhabitants of the city and neighbourhood.'

In 1771 he sent Sathyanadhan, a trusted and devoted catechist, to live in Tinnevelly and begin work there; he himself visited the neighbourhood twice. The district of Tinnevelly, the southernmost in the peninsula of South India, was to prove one of the most fruitful fields for missionary work; and we owe all the subsequent great harvest to the foresight of this supreme genius. Fully convinced of the rich possibilities of that area, the S.P.C.K. sent out in the year 1788 the Rev. R. D. Jænicke, who, after acquiring a knowledge of Tamil in Tranquebar, proceeded to Tinnevelly as the first missionary to that district. At the end of 1780, Sathyanadhan was ordained, and between them Jænicke and Sathyanadhan were responsible for the beginning of the great movement which has led to the present number of about three hundred thousand Christians.

After nearly half a century of glorious work for the Master, Schwartz was called to his rest on February the 13th, 1789, aged seventy-one. At this time the total number of Christian adherents connected with the Danish mission was about twenty thousand. Two monuments were erected to his memory, one at Madras in St. Mary's Church by the S.P.C.K. and the other (executed by the sculptor Flaxman) by Raja Serfogee in the Fort Church in Tanjore.

The last few years of the eighteenth century were marked by trouble between the Tranquebar Government and the missionaries, and there was much confusion and a decline of the work. To quote Dr. Warneck, 'Amid various little strifes and ample distress, this on the whole solid and not unfruitful mission maintained itself until, in the last quarter of the century and afterwards, rationalism at home dug up its roots. The universities, having fallen completely under the sway of this withering movement, ceased to furnish theologians. Meanwhile, a more living interest had been awakened in England, and so the connection which had already for some time existed with friends of missions there, and especially the alliance with the church missionary societies, saved the Tamil Mission from ruin.' The centenary celebrations of the Tranquebar Mission were carried through in a very half-hearted manner: 'The consequences are,' said the missionaries writing in 1807, ' that we have become almost desponding, that our churches are empty and that baptism and the Lord's supper are despised.'

After the taking of Tranquebar by the English in February 1808 the Mission further declined, and the chapter which had begun in such glorious self-sacrifice and devotion ended somewhat shamefacedly with the Mission giving up all its work to the S.P.C.K. in May 1820.

But these pioneers of Protestant missionary work in the East had done gloriously for the Lord and had built better than they knew. The methods they devised—the initial acquisition of proficiency in the local vernaculars, the translation of the Scriptures in the local language, their printing and wide distribution, the composition of a vernacular hymnology, schools for children, both English and vernacular, itinerant preaching, discussions with the religious leaders of the non-Christian communities, establishment of a lay ministry of teachers and catechists, the ordination of the best educated and most capable among the converts and passing on the responsibility for pastoral superintendence of congregations to their hands—these and similar methods of these pioneers have been the foundation principles of missionary work ever since. They rightly conceived their mission as not to baptize but to convert the heathen, and were not content with any conversion that was not genuine. They gave a prolonged course of instruction to catechumens preparatory to baptism and did not admit any one to the sacrament unless he had shown signs of a real change of heart and was seen to be of an upright moral conduct. Faced at every turn with the intolerance of the Hindu priestly hierarchy, the enmity of their Roman catholic co-missionaries and the immorality of the European laity, they overcame these obstacles by maintaining a very high standard in their own lives and demanding from their converts an equally high standard as far as circumstances permitted. The Church in India owes an inestimable debt of gratitude to this noble-hearted band of early Protestant missionaries.

IV

THE BEGINNINGS OF
THE ENTERPRISE IN NORTH INDIA

For a full two hundred years after the incorporation of the East India Company on December the 31st, 1600, Britain did not wake up to its responsibility for offering the blessings of Christianity to the people of the country from which it was deriving so much wealth. The sole object of the company of merchants chartered under the title of 'The Governour and company of Merchants of London trading in the East Indies' was the exchange of goods between England and the East Indies. That by a series of fortuitous circumstances this Company should have come into possession of vast territories which they were compelled to govern to the satisfaction of the Government at home and that they should have become if not actually the instruments at least the means for the spread of the gospel in India is one of the clearest proofs of the intervening providence of God in the affairs of men.

The first traces of a concern for propagating Christianity among the heathen are seen in the charter of September the 5th, 1698, in which provision was made not only for a minister in every garrison and superior factory in the East Indies and for a place set apart for divine service, but also that the 'ministers as shall be sent to reside in India shall be obliged to learn, within one year of their arrival, the Portuguese language, and shall apply themselves to learn the native language of the country where they shall reside, the better to enable them to instruct the Gentoos, that shall be servants or slaves of the same Company or of their agents, in the Protestant Religion'. But little was done by the Company itself to give effect to these provisions. Places of worship of some kind had existed in the three principal settlements before the 1698 charter. The first English church to be built in India was the Church of St. Mary the Virgin, built in Fort St. George in 1678 by Streynsham Master, the Governor, mainly at his own expense. John Evans, the first chaplain to the Bay, found a chapel for his ministrations when he arrived there in 1678. But throughout its whole history the East India Company spent very little of its revenues on building churches.

The period between the 1698 charter and the last decade of the eighteenth century witnessed the most phenomenal expansion of the East India Company. Vast territories were acquired, its civil and military personnel increased enormously, commerce flourished, and throughout the whole occupied area it assumed governing and administrative powers. During this immense expansion the establishment of chaplains was considerably enlarged, though the official policy towards missionary work continued unchanged. The Company steadfastly refused to sponsor active evangelistic work, or to permit its chaplains to do anything of that kind. During the major part of the first half of the nineteenth century it even refused permission to missionaries to enter its territories for work.

In the meanwhile, there were being released among the people of Britain spiritual forces which awakened the English Church to its duty to the people who had been brought under the Government's care through the activities of the East India Company. About the end of the seventeenth century the Society for Promoting Christian Knowledge and the Society for the Propagation of the Gospel in Foreign parts came into being and received their charters. Throughout the eighteenth century the tide of religious life in England and in Protestant Europe continued steadily to rise, and this was evidenced by the large number of missionary societies which came into existence.

The honour of sending the first English missionary to India belongs, however, to the Baptist Church in England. As early as 1784, a few Baptist ministers were meeting regularly for united prayer for the revival of religion and the extension of the Redeemer's kingdom, and William Carey of Moulton in Northamptonshire was being prepared by God for the great work of taking the Gospel to heathen lands. The publication of his *An Enquiry into the Obligations of Christians to use Means for the Conversion of the Heathen*, and the sermon he preached from Isa. 54. 2, 3, which he ended with his two famous exhortations, ' Attempt great things for God; expect great things from God ', led to the formation of the Baptist Missionary Society at Kettering on the 2nd of October 1792. John Thomas, a Baptist surgeon on an Indiaman plying between England and India, who had just come back from India with a passion for the evangelization of the country, having himself made small beginnings in that direction, offered to return to Bengal as its missionary, and as a colleague of William Carey, who had also offered to go out to India.

On June the 13th, 1793, they sailed from England on a Danish East Indiaman and arrived in Calcutta on November 11th. Carey and Thomas were, however, forbidden by the Company to establish a mission in Calcutta. Their engagement with the Society whose funds were inadequate to support them was that they were to maintain themselves. Thomas was prepared to practise his profession. Carey had to look out for some employment to support his wife and four children. He accepted employment as superintendent of an indigo factory in a place called Mudnabatty near Malda on a salary of £300 a year. This, however, did not prevent his doing the work for which he had expressly come out. He used the six years spent in this place to learn Bengali, and to translate the Scriptures into that language. All the time he also preached to the non-Christians and started a school.

Carey and Thomas were joined by the Rev. John Fountain, and in October 1799 by four young missionaries, Messrs. William Ward, Daniel Brundson, William Grant and Joshua Marshman. (In a few days Grant was removed by death.) They arrived in an American ship: and had not obtained any permission or licence from the Court of Directors. They were, therefore, suspect, and the Government officials in Calcutta opposed their landing and wanted to send them back to

England. But they escaped to Serampore, fifteen miles from Calcutta, a Danish settlement, where the Danish Governor gave them protection and encouraged them to begin their work. There they remained till 1800 when Carey was also persuaded to leave Malda and join them. Thenceforth Serampore became the headquarters of the Baptist Mission. Never have men devoted themselves more wholeheartedly to the work of evangelization than they. Their first aim was the printing of the Scriptures in the native languages. Carey had translated both the Testaments; the presses and types were ready and Ward had all the knowledge of a first-rate printer. So, whilst Carey went out into the highways to preach, Ward and Marshman, studying hard at the vernacular languages of the country, undertook to set up the New Testament in good Bengali; and on the 18th of May 1800, to the inexpressible joy of the whole party, the first sheet was struck off. In less than a year from that date, on the 7th of February 1801, the whole of the New Testament had been printed in Bengali.

The first fruit of their evangelistic labours was the conversion of a Bengali carpenter named Krishna Pal who was baptized on the last Sunday of the year 1800. Other successes came, though very slowly. At the end of 1802 they had only thirteen communicants and nine inquirers. Early in 1803 they gained their first convert from the great sacerdotal caste of Brahmins, a young man named Soroop. He and all the converts were subjected to great persecution by their Hindu relatives and fellow caste people. Whenever they appeared in the streets they were hooted at and insulted and not infrequently violently assaulted. They were not given houses to live in and were molested in every way possible.

In 1803 the missionaries were reinforced by the arrival of Mr. and Mrs. Chamberlain, and two years later of four new missionaries, Messrs. Biss, Mardon, Moor and Rowe. The translation of the Bible into more of the vernaculars occupied the main attention of the senior missionaries. But they also went out in batches on preaching tours during which they distributed thousands of tracts. Even though the mission could not claim to have made numerous conversions, it supplied the means of converting nearly the whole Oriental world. Gospels in Malay were published and a translation into Chinese begun.

In the year 1806 their hands were further strengthened by the arrival of some young chaplains of the East India Company's establishment. The spread of Christianity in North India owes a very great deal to the work of this group of Evangelical clergy who came out as chaplains of the East India Company. While the Baptist missionaries were confined to Serampore, these chaplains, posted to different places in North India, were able to spread the Gospel much further. Fired with a passion for evangelism they all began definite missionary work long before the Anglican Church sent out missionaries. Each of them had heard the missionary call; but because the East India Company was at this time most averse to direct missionary efforts they could only come out as chaplains and hope to fulfil their desire. Being men of exemplary character and marked piety, they tried by word and deed, at least partially succeeding, to Christianize their own countrymen in India whose impious living was a great obstruction to the cause of the Gospel.

Of the several who thus came out five are most outstanding —David Brown, Claudius Buchanan, Henry Martyn, Daniel Corrie and I. T. Thompson. But the greatest of them all was Henry Martyn—though all of them, in addition to their own work as chaplains, worked among the people, preaching to them, holding discussions with Hindu and Muslim leaders and establishing schools.

The formation of the Church Missionary Society in England may be said to have been due to the ideas which first took shape in David Brown's mind. Brown, Grant and Udny met together and worked out a scheme which they sent to their friends in London and Cambridge. The Church Missionary Society was inaugurated in London in 1799; but its birthplace may be said to be the old Mission Church in Calcutta and David Brown the true father of it.

To Claudius Buchanan the Church in India owes a great deal. He was the first to suggest the need of an Ecclesiastical

Establishment. He was the one to bring to the notice of the Western Church the needs of the Syrian Church in Travancore by means of his researches into the work of the Christian Church in Asia. He retired after twelve years in India.

The most remarkable of all these chaplains was Henry Martyn. A distinguished classical scholar and a brilliant mathematician (he was senior wrangler and Fellow of St. John's College, Cambridge), he did more for the cause of missionary work in India during his short life than any missionary save St. Francis Xavier. He came to India partly because he was fired —as were all the other four of this group of chaplains—with the spark of missionary zeal by the Rev. Charles Simeon, Vicar of Holy Trinity, Cambridge, and partly because of what he had heard of Carey's wonderful work in India. On the voyage out he studied Sanskrit, Persian and Arabic. He arrived on May the 16th, 1806; and his famous ' I have hitherto lived to little purpose, like a clod upon the earth. Now let me burn out for God ' occurs in his diary for May the 17th.

Martyn remained in Calcutta for the first six months and was thereafter posted to Dinapore in the province of Behar, west of Patna, as chaplain to the two regiments stationed there. Here, in addition to his own work, preaching to non-Christians and holding daily discussions with Hindus and Mohammedans, he spent a great deal of his time translating the New Testament into Urdu, which he completed in March 1808. ' Probably, next to his devoted life, this piece of work was his greatest contribution to the cause of Christianity in India.' He also prepared a book on the parables of our Lord and a translation of the Book of Common Prayer. From Dinapore he was transferred to Cawnpore, where there was no church and where he had to conduct services for the European troops in the open air. This affected his health seriously and he soon became a victim to malaria. The work which was nearest his heart was evangelistic work among Indians. In spite of all difficulties and opposition, he managed to start schools (as he had done also in Dinapore) and translated for their use into the local dialect his book on the parables. He also began Persian and Arabic versions of the New Testament. Here it was that

Abdul Maseeh was converted as a result of Henry Martyn's preaching and influence. Daniel Corrie, who had been appointed in 1810 to Agra, stayed at Cawnpore with Henry Martyn on his way to his new destination, and was shocked to find him so greatly run down in health. He persuaded him to go to Calcutta for a change and to undertake a sea voyage. It was clear that Martyn was suffering from incipient consumption.

On the last Sunday of September 1810 he took leave of his European congregation in Cawnpore. On that very day the new building for which he had been responsible was opened for divine service. It became the military church and was in use till it was destroyed in 1857 during the Mutiny. He left Cawnpore on October the 1st for Calcutta, having decided to go to England via Persia. He remained in Calcutta for about two months, embarking on the 7th of January for Bombay, intending to go on to Arabia and Persia, as he was anxious to finalize his translation of the Scriptures into Arabic and Persian. He reached Shiraz, where he completed the translation of the Bible into Persian. He then travelled from Shiraz to Ispahan and thence to Teheran and Tocat, all on horseback. Ten days before his death he wrote in wistful mood, ' I sat in the orchard and thought with what sweet comfort and peace of my God, in solitude my company, my Friend and Comforter. O when shall time give place to eternity? When shall appear that new heaven and new earth wherein dwelleth righteousness? ' He died on the 16th of October 1812, aged only thirty-two years. ' Of all the men who had gone before him on the same Christian enterprise, Xavier alone can be compared with him in intensity of zeal and heroism of character. In both was there the same burning love of their fellow men, the same eager spirit of adventure, the same vast power of self-annihilation, the same ecstatic communion with the unseen world. Both died with the harness on their backs, far from home and all friendly succour, broken down by much fatigue and much suffering. And whether we look upon the picture of the gaunt Jesuit, stretched beneath a wretched shed on the barren coast of Sancian breathing out his soul with uplifted eyes in accents of hope and adoration, or watch over Martyn's dying bed, as, plague-stricken, he lay at Tocat with his Bible by his side—we still see the grandest of human spectacles, the triumph of the spirit over the flesh.'[1]

Daniel Corrie arrived in Calcutta a few months later than Henry Martyn. He was destined to give over thirty years of his life to India and to finish his career as the first Bishop of Madras. The day was now approaching when India was really to be thrown open to missionary enterprise. As the time for a fresh revision of the Company's charter came near, Wilberforce, strongly supported by the S.P.C.K. and the C.M.S., tried to secure this privilege through Parliament, though he had failed at the time of the previous revision. Once more the House of Commons was treated by the opponents of Christian work to a glowing description of Hinduism and its 'benignant and softening influences' and to expressions of 'horror at the idea of sending out Baptists and Anabaptists to convert such a people, disturbing institutions ordained by Providence to make them virtuous and happy'. But this time Wilberforce succeeded. Two resolutions were moved and carried. One acknowledged 'our duty to promote the interests and happiness of the Indian peoples' and that, with a view to the introduction of 'useful knowledge and religious and moral improvement', 'sufficient facilities should be afforded by law to persons desirous of going to and remaining in India' to accomplish 'these benevolent designs'. The other resolution provided for the establishment of a bishopric in Calcutta with three archdeacons. This was not seriously opposed in Parliament, though the usual objection was raised that the time was 'not opportune'. The Bill received the royal assent on July the 21st, 1813.

This provision in the charter for the promotion of Christianity soon began to bear fruit. By the month of June the first Bishop of Calcutta, Dr. Middleton, was on his way out. Other missionary societies were also stimulated to send out missionaries to India, e.g., the C.M.S., who planted a mission in Calcutta in 1815 at Kidderpur, and the London Missionary Society which had sent its first missionary, Mr. Forsyth, to India in

[1] Kaye: *Christianity in India*, p. 213.

1798; he had established himself under the protection of the liberal Dutch Government at Chinsurah, twenty miles north of Calcutta.

Bishop Middleton's first important act was to set up a Calcutta Diocesan committee in connection with the S.P.C.K., which did good work distributing Bibles, tracts, prayer-books and other religious literature, and also established schools. He began the Bishop's College, the main object of which was to prepare Christian youth as preachers, catechists and school-masters. The foundation stone was laid on the 15th of December 1820. The college was completed after several years and placed under the control of the S.P.G. It has made a great contribution to the work of the Church in India, and has been for some time the premier Anglican Theological College in the East.

The Serampore mission continued its manifold enterprises with undiminished vigour. The Serampore College was established in 1818. The King of Denmark, with his accustomed generosity, presented the missionaries with a valuable estate, the rent of which was to be appropriated to the expenses of the college. He also granted them a royal charter of Incorporation giving the college the privilege and authority of conferring literary and honorary degrees.

By 1826, the learned Baptist missionaries had translated and printed the whole of the Bible in five of the languages of India and the New Testament in fifteen others. In six other languages it was more than half printed and in ten others considerable progress had been made. These vast undertakings had been accomplished within the short space of thirty years since the first translation—the New Testament in Bengali. ' Carey laid the foundations broad and deep of the great Protestant missionary movement not only in India but in all the Orient. For forty-one years, unbroken by return to England, he toiled for India's Christian conquest, his death occurring on June 9th, 1834. Surely William Carey not only attempted but accomplished great things for God; he expected and received great things from God.'[1]

[1] Bishop J. M. Thoburn, *The Christian Conquest of India*, p. 144.

By the time of the Sepoy mutiny practically the whole of northern and western India had been occupied by missions; and when once the shock of the mutiny had subsided, there followed a wonderful half-century of achievement.

V

CAMPAIGNING METHODS

THE history of the modern Christian enterprise in India can be divided into five periods.

The first was the period of pioneering—the period of tentative efforts, experimentation with methods and agencies—characterized by a certain hesitation and working against great odds in the face of opposition from several quarters, a period when tools and weapons were being invented and forged—the translation of the Scriptures into the main vernaculars, and the provision of forms of worship, of a hymnology and rudimentary devotional literature for the use of new converts. This may be said to have lasted till the year 1813 when the restrictions against missionaries and the direct obstructions from high places to missionary work were removed. This threw open the way for the arrival of Christian forces from the west in large numbers and the gradual occupation of the country by missionary agencies.

The next period, which lasted till the Sepoy mutiny, was a period of settling down. The different missionary societies confined their activities to specified areas and made room by reducing their frontiers for new societies to come in. The work was, however, characterized by strong individualism. Communication with the home society being difficult and uncertain, the missionary was left free to make his own decisions and his own experiments.

The third period began in 1858, when the Government of the country passed into the hands of the Queen of England and her Parliament, and lasted for fifty years. This synchronized with political, intellectual and religious revival and with active opposition—this time from the intelligentsia of the country—to Christian work. This was also the time when Hinduism and Hindu society were profoundly affected and changed by the impact of the Christian religion and its culture from the west.

The fourth period may be said to have begun with the Edinburgh Conference of 1910, and lasted till the country became independent. It was a period of the growth of the Church in India as a young church—one of the ' younger churches ' represented at Jerusalem and Tambaram—a period characterized by a gradual revision by missionary societies of their conception of their status and purpose. We find Indians more and more closely associated with Europeans on equal terms, taking their place in the highest councils of the missions and of the Churches. The missionary motive itself changed. It was not so much working to save the heathen from damnation as planting and establishing churches and helping them through educational and medical facilities to preach a gospel leading to a more abundant life. This was the time when movements toward organic union began and a sense of a national Christian movement, focused in the National Christian Council or its provincial or regional councils, was created.

The fifth period has just begun. The political independence of the country has profoundly affected the whole situation. The western missionary has had to give up his adventitious and in most cases un-asked-for superiority along with his civilian contemporaries. Missions are giving place to the Indian Church: for in the new India missions may be just tolerated while the Indian Church, being an integral part of the nation, will be wanted and appreciated, as long as it carries out its Christian ministry and makes its Christian contribution to the national life. Henceforward the Indian Church will be responsible for the whole of the Christian enterprise in the country. In South India a new organically united Church has come into being and it is a good augury. But even where such an organic union has not taken place, there is closer co-operation between the different denominations, which are indeed no longer denominations but small indigenous churches themselves. A policy of devolution is being increasingly followed, along with greater integration of the mission and the Church. Missions are gradually handing over their functions to the Church and are practically disappearing, not by ceasing to exist, but by being absorbed. Leadership is becoming increasingly Indian. Christian thinking and planning in the community is becoming more and more church-led, not missionary-led. It is quite obvious that in God's good time there will be more and more organic union between the different Churches in the country.

In the last four chapters we have had glimpses into the romantic beginnings of the Christian enterprise. It is impossible to attempt to give even a short summary of its history in this vast country during the succeeding period of one hundred and fifty years. But an attempt may be made to study the development of new missionary methods to suit changing conditions. Itinerant preaching and vernacular schools were the only methods used during the first fifty years of the Christian enterprise in this country: but, later, other methods such as high schools and colleges, medical work and women's work came to be employed.

William Carey, the great pioneer, had thought even of high schools as he thought of almost every other good plan subsequently widely adopted. In 1818 he founded in Serampore a college for the 'instruction of Asiatic Christians and other youth in Eastern literature and European Science'. But the system owes its reputation and permanence to the fine work of the Scottish missionaries. Alexander Duff seems to have been specially prepared by God for this very purpose, that of establishing Christian higher education as a potent factor in the evangelization of the country.

He was born in 1806. Graduating from St. Andrew's, he was ordained and soon offered himself for missionary work in India. After two shipwrecks he arrived with his young wife in Calcutta on May the 27th, 1830. A man of commanding presence, unbounded zeal and energy and full of original ideas, he found in William Carey a guide whose help was invaluable. Very soon it became plain to him that what he had been sent out by God to accomplish was to meet what was then perhaps the most crying need in the country, a Christian mission college which should do its work with the English language as its medium, open the treasures of English literature to Indian minds, bring them into contact with western philosophy and western science, and, most of all, imbue them with a knowledge of the message of Christianity and bring to them news of the love and saving power of Jesus Christ. He carried out his scheme in the face of much opposition from missionary circles and with the help of some influential Hindu gentlemen, and effected a revolution in the educational methods of missionary societies. The successful work of the college led to the plan being adopted in other big cities of India by the Scottish Missionary Society, by other societies, and eventually by the British Government in India.

In March 1835 Lord William Bentinck, the Governor-General in Council, decided to change the whole system which had prevailed in government institutions for about fifteen years. He directed that henceforth the funds appropriated to education should be employed chiefly in imparting to the indigenous population a knowledge of European literature and science through the medium of the English language, and that in every government institution boys of every caste should be admitted without distinction. Both these changes were the direct result of the principles followed by Alexander Duff in his college, where his efforts were directed towards the production of high character and towards the emancipation of young Hindus from the intellectual shackles of their own religion. Such an effort was most urgently needed to counteract the evil effects of the government institutions which were producing a very undesirable type of student who were almost atheists and whose energies were directed towards destruction of all that was good even in their own culture and religion. Its first most noticeable effect was seen in the large numbers of high-caste Hindus who were drawn to the school and from whose ranks some were soon led to Christ, such as Krishna Mohun Bannerjee, Gopinath Nundy, Anando Chunder Mozumdar and Lal Behari Dey. No less than forty-eight young men of the higher castes were led to accept Christ as their Saviour through the influence of Duff and his college. ' While you are separating precious atoms from the mass we shall prepare a mine which shall explode one day and by God's blessing tear up the whole,' said Dr. Duff in answer to his critics; and while it may be that the formidable mass of Hinduism has not yet been blown up, yet it has been so completely undermined that what now stands is but a hollow shell. There are to-day in the country over thirty colleges, over two hundred and fifty high schools, nearly five hundred middle schools and about fourteen hundred primary schools run under Christian auspices.

Medical missions, though principally works of mercy and not primarily evangelistic, have again and again been the means of opening the door for the spread of the Gospel. Our Lord not only taught the people but healed their diseases as well. In India there is so little medical help and government efforts are so inadequate that the Christian missionary must come to the Government's help, just as he has done in the field of education. Their value as an adjunct to more direct work is now fully realized: but it was not till comparatively late that they were adopted as a missionary method. Regular hospitals and dispensaries are of course quite modern; but almost from the very beginning there was a little occasional medical work accompanying purely evangelistic work.

It was to the first medical missionary, Mr. Thomas, the erstwhile surgeon of an East India Company's merchantman, that we owe the conversion of the first Hindu in Bengal who had the courage to be baptized, Krishna Pal, a carpenter living in Serampore, whom he cured of a dislocation of the shoulder. The first Indian helper whom the first two Lutheran missionaries to Tranquebar had in the year 1714 also owed his conversion to the fact that he was first medically treated by them. Abdul Maseeh, at Agra, became widely known as the ' Christian Hakim ', as he supplemented his preaching by spending half his stipend in procuring medicines and healing hundreds of sick folk. The native State of Jeypore, a great stronghold of Hinduism, where no missionary was permitted to settle, was thrown open to Christian work solely because Dr. Valentine, while passing through Jeypore, treated the Maharani who was very ill, and whom the native physicians had given up. Through God's blessing she was restored to health by means of Dr. Valentine's treatment. The Maharajah then invited Dr. Valentine to stay on as his private physician. He agreed upon one condition, that he should be allowed to preach the Gospel without let or hindrance. The Maharajah agreed, and Dr. Valentine remained at Jeypore for fourteen years, till it became the centre of a prosperous mission of the Presbyterian Church.

The S.P.G. was the first missionary society to employ missionaries with medical qualifications; and the first qualified medical missionary to come out to India was their missionary in Tinnevelly, the Rev. J. M. Strachan, M.D., of Edinburgh, who came out in 1861. His work was found to be of immense value during the epidemic of cholera which raged in those parts in the year 1865. He opened a regular mission hospital in Nazareth in 1870: which soon produced magnificent results, disarming opposition and overcoming prejudice. When he left to become the Bishop of Rangoon, the work was carried on by the Rev. A. Margoschis and the hospital at Nazareth became the nucleus of a network of small hospitals and dispensaries which were established throughout the district.

The need for medical relief for women in India is even greater than for men. Mrs. Winter of the S.P.G. had already begun in 1863 medical work of a simple kind in the zenanas in Delhi, which became a distinctive feature of the whole mission there. But it was at the beginning of 1870 that there came to India a woman pioneer in medical missionary work, Clara Swain, an American missionary of the Methodist Episcopal Church, who founded the first hospital in India for women in Bareilly in the United Provinces. Since then mission hospitals have grown wonderfully in number and in influence. There is practically no mission which does not maintain one or more. There are now about three hundred mission hospitals and about seven hundred dispensaries with three hundred foreign doctors and five hundred Indian doctors. Some have become famous throughout the land and medical work has called forth the disinterested sacrificial service of hundreds of Christian medical men and women of all races.

Medical work is one of the most effective evangelistic agencies that are now in use. It enables the Church to get contacts with a large number of people who would otherwise not be touched at all, and to influence them in favour of the Gospel not by its direct preaching but by demonstration of what is undoubtedly its outstanding characteristic, namely love. It uses a method hallowed by our Lord Himself and seeks to help men and women in the hour of their greatest physical and spiritual need.

In the year 1834 the American missionary, Mr. Abeel, went to England and pleaded the cause of 'Female Missions', pointing out the imperative need for work among women as well as men in Oriental countries. In response to his appeal was founded a Society for Promoting Female Education in the East, later named 'the Indian Female Normal School and Instruction Society'. As early as 1820 Miss Cooke had come out and had started girls' schools in Calcutta and for several years the Society confined its attention to schools and did not think of any other form of direct evangelistic work, though several of the ladies who came out under the auspices of the Society did not, in fact, confine their work to schools. Through the children they reached the mothers. A Miss Toogood, an English teacher in the normal school for training Eurasian teachers in Calcutta, was the first to succeed in entering the zenana of a wealthy Hindu family in that city, in the year 1854.

In 1831 the American mission in Ahmednagar tried the experiment of employing Indian Christian bible-women by sending groups of them on preaching tours. They travelled in a cart from village to village, preaching and talking to women in their homes. This had a great effect in interesting the women, especially of the higher castes, in Christianity.

When, in 1842, a lady offered to work among women in India, Bishop Wilson replied, 'I object on principle to single ladies coming out unprotected to so distant a place with a climate so unfriendly, and with the almost certainty of their marrying within a month of their arrival. I imagine the beloved Persis, Tryphena, Tryphosa, Julia and others who laboured much in the Lord, remained in their own neighbourhoods and families.' But the clamant need of India's women was forcing itself upon the attention of all interested in the evangelization of the country: and in the year 1861 the first step was taken by the I.F.N.S.I.S[1], to send out English ladies definitely for zenana visiting and teaching. In 1863, Mrs. Winter introduced the zenana system in Delhi. Bishop Milman was convinced that 'without the education and enlightenment of the female sex the difficulties of gospel work and the conversion of Hindus and Mohammedans seem almost insuperable'. From that time progress was steady, especially after the formation of the Church of England Zenana Missionary Society in 1880. Among the many devoted women who came out was Miss Charlotte Tucker, the A.L.O.E.[2] of young people's literature, who laboured as an honorary missionary for eighteen years and died in 1893 in her post at Batala in the Punjab. Another lady, Miss Beilby, seems to have been the first to engage definitely in medical work, beginning in 1876 at Lucknow, where in her first year she paid over a thousand visits in a hundred and fifty houses, besides seeing other patients in her own house. One of the Christian Indian helpers was Miss Golak Nath, daughter of a highly respected minister of the American Presbyterian Mission, who became the wife of the Rajah of Kapurthala, Sir Harnam Singh.

Gradually women missionaries came to engage themselves in all branches of work among women. Zenana visiting, high schools for girls, boarding schools for Christian girls, women teacher-training institutions, bible-women, zenana hospitals, the training of nurses—all came to be the special concern of women missionaries. Conditions in India have considerably changed: house-to-house visiting in order to meet the ladies of the household is no longer possible and in any case cannot be as fruitful as it once was. But the need for work of other kinds among women, especially in rural areas, is as great as ever.

In India, women exercise tremendous religious influence at home. It is they who see that the family gods are daily worshipped and who teach even the children in arms to worship

[1] See above.
[2] A.L.O.E. (A Lady of England) was Charlotte Tucker's *nom de plume*.

them. It is they who see that the ever-recurring festivals are observed, that the birth, marriage and funeral rites are duly performed; that caste is not broken. It is the influence of wife and mother that keeps multitudes of men who are convinced of the truth of Christianity from publicly acknowledging it. To win the women would be to win India.

No picture of the Christian enterprise in India at this period will be complete unless the facts regarding the official connection which the British Government in India long maintained with organized Hinduism are at least briefly mentioned. For a very long time the Government not only encouraged the perpetuation of Hinduism in all its aspects, but also placed every obstacle in the way of the progress of Christianity, especially by refusing to give the new convert to the faith a fair deal, subjecting him to all kinds of uncalled-for handicaps.

It was the Madras Government which commenced it, and it was in that presidency that the practice was carried to its utmost limit; but the evil, once begun, spread also to the other presidencies. The Government appropriated the revenues of the temples arising from villages and lands, and also the gifts and offerings of the worshippers, levied taxes from the pilgrims, and, in return, provided, from the revenues, for the maintenance of the temples and the temple worship. In some cases, where the temple did not get enough income of its own, it made grants from the treasury for the purpose, and even presented gifts and offerings to the idols in the name of the Company. Nor was this all. The servants of the Company were required to attend Hindu and Mohammedan festivals, as a mark of respect. Festivals in the temples were carried on under official supervision, and government servants were made responsible for the administration of temple revenues, the performance of all ceremonies, the appointment of priests and attendants and even the prostitutes of the temple. The military, under the command of English officers, were required to attend on the great Hindu festivals, partly to preserve order, but partly also to add to their pomp and show. Even at the more ordinary Hindu and Mohammedan festivals, royal salutes were fired. Several servants of the Company whose Christian principles would not allow them to take part in such functions—such as Sir Peregrine Maitland, Commander-in-Chief of the Madras Army, and Mr. R. Nelson of the Madras Civil Service—resigned valuable appointments rather than be guilty of such a dereliction of moral and religious duty.

When this official connection of the Government in India with Hinduism came to be widely known in England, efforts were made to put an end to this evil custom, and the matter was taken up by the directors of the Company. In February 1833, a despatch was sent to the Governor-General, directing that the interference of British officials in the management of Hindu temples should cease. But the authorities in India were indifferent and the despatch remained for a long time a dead letter.

In 1840, peremptory orders were sent out to put an end at once to any connection, on the part of the Company's officers, troops and servants, with processions or other religious ceremonies. But the Madras Government obstinately adhered to the practice. In 1844, the directors had to send out yet another despatch ordering the complete discontinuance of the interference of the Government in such concerns. Even so, it took another eighteen years before the Governments of India completely severed their connection with Hindu temples. The last temple was not handed over till 1862.

The Government did not only thus support Hinduism, but was adverse to the acceptance of the new faith by Indians. The ancient Hindu and Mohammedan laws, by which anyone renouncing those faiths was deprived of all his rights to family property and even to his own self-acquired property, were rigorously enforced against every convert.

Not only that. The Government did itself issue orders discriminating heavily against those Indians who embraced Christianity. It made judicial regulations by which *moonsifs* (judges of considerable status and responsibility) and also *vakeels* (legal practitioners) were required to be of the Hindu or Mohammedan religion, thus practically excluding Indian Christians from some of the most important and lucrative professions open to them. In the army, though there was no positive law affecting Christian converts, yet the prevailing rule was that the untouchable classes should not be enlisted even for the ranks. Christians were classified as untouchables, and were excluded from the army. It was long before anything was done to mitigate this oppression.

It was in April 1850 that the Earl of Dalhousie, the Governor-General in Council, enacted that 'so much of any law or usage in force within the British territories as inflicts on any person forfeiture of rights or property, or may be held in any way to impair or affect any right of inheritance by reason of his or her renouncing or having been excluded from the communion of any religion, or being deprived of caste, shall cease to be enforced as law in the courts of East India Company, and in the courts established by Royal Charter within the said territories'. It was then that the charter of religious liberty was established in India, and universal toleration became the law for the whole country. Christianity for the first time got a fair deal.

VI

SOME HEROES OF THE INDIAN CHURCH

EVERY living Church from the very beginnings of Christianity has produced a large number of outstanding heroes whose privilege it was to suffer for their faith, not a martyr's death, but daily martyrdom under persecution, opposition and ignominy. Not all of them are famous in Christian history. And so in India while we have had in many a town and village dotted all over the country, ever since Christianity came to it, simple, humble, holy people of whom the world knows nothing, pastors in lonely out-stations, teachers, workers and just ordinary Christians who 'do the day's work and shine as they do it'; we have also had a remarkably large number of veritable heroes of the Cross, some rising to distinguished leadership in the Church, others living and suffering in their lowly stations and being used wonderfully by God for the extension of His Kingdom. Their lives give us a true picture of the conditions under which Christ's Kingdom grew in this land. Four of them selected at random are presented below as samples of different types which Indian Christianity has produced:

I. RAJA NAIKEN

The Soldier-Evangelist

From the very beginning 'God hath chosen the foolish things of the world to confound the wise and things which are despised hath God chosen to bring to nought things that are '.

This was well exemplified in the life of Rajanaiken and his great work for the extension of God's Kingdom in the very earliest days of Christianity in South India.

Ever since missionary work had begun in Tranquebar, the Danish missionaries were desirous of occupying the adjacent kingdom of Tanjore for Christ, but the Raja refused to allow any European missionary to enter. Ziegenbalg, putting on Indian dress, made an attempt in 1709, but was detected and sent back. Within a few years, however, the Raja was won over, partly by the earnestness and exemplary character of the Danish missionaries, but partly also because of the good offices of Rajanaiken, who was an under-officer in his service and who, after having been converted to the Roman Catholic faith, later gave up that communion and joined the Lutherans. Relinquishing his military career, he entered the service of the mission and served it for more than forty years as a catechist. Thus, a poor outcaste pariah, an untouchable, was the one who opened the way of the Gospel into the kingdom of Tanjore.

Born of Roman Catholic parents, his grandfather having joined the Roman Church, he was sent to school, where he learned to read and write Tamil and later joined the Raja's army. He was anxious to read the Bible, but no Roman Catholic translation of the Scriptures into Tamil existed. By chance he acquired the four Gospels and the Acts which had been printed in Tranquebar in 1714 (being Part I of Ziegenbalg's translation of the New Testament) and, as he wrote later, 'My longing was satisfied with it. I used to read it all day and then from evening till midnight by light. It poured like oil upon my faith and caused it to burn brightly. I then went myself to Tranquebar with my brothers, visited the priests and received the whole of the New Testament.' (As a matter of fact, it was God's providential leading that took him to the neighbourhood of Tranquebar, as head of a detachment of soldiers sent by the Raja to protect the crops, at a time of great distress owing to extensive floods, famine and widespread robberies of grain.) 'Moreover, I had the opportunity of talking with them on the difference between the Romish and the Evangelical creeds. After I had had about six months intercourse with them, partly in writing, partly by word of mouth, and had studied the Bible after I returned to Tanjore, the evangelical texts which shine like stars in heaven had awakened and strengthened me. I was thereby persuaded to leave the Roman Church. When I returned to Tranquebar in 1728 I joined the Evangelical congregation.'

Having thus seen the truth, he was anxious to communicate it to others and began to teach the soldiers under him. He was thrilled when he found that the Tamil word used for 'centurion' in the tenth chapter of Acts was *servaikaran*, his own rank in the army; and he determined to follow the example of the God-fearing centurion Cornelius. One summer, he came to Tranquebar with three of his soldiers whom he had himself taught and who, having given up the worship of idols, wished to be baptized. The missionaries instructed these catechumens further in the faith and eventually baptized them.

In the same year, 1727, at the request of Rajanaiken, Catechist Aaron was sent to Tanjore with a letter and some small presents from the missionaries to the Prince, who received him very kindly, and invited the missionaries to visit him at Vyteesurenkoil, a small town about a day's journey north-west of Tranquebar, where he was soon to attend the big annual festival in the Hindu temple there. In the year 1728, M. Pressier accompanied by Aaron met the Prince, who permitted him to address large gatherings of Brahmins and other learned Hindus, and also to preach in the villages near by. Thus was the way opened for the Christian enterprise in the kingdom of Tanjore.

The Roman Catholic priests never forgave Rajanaiken his secession from their Church. They were further incensed when they saw him converting several to the Evangelical faith and began to persecute him. The success which attended his labours in the cause of Christ induced Rajanaiken to quit the army and devote himself entirely to the service of the Lord. He therefore left the Raja's service and went to the missionaries at Tranquebar, who, being quite satisfied with his integrity and knowing how much it had cost him to give up his remunerative military employment, had no hesitation in accept-

C

ing him and, after commissioning him at a special service, sent him to labour in the kingdom of Tanjore which he had opened for God's work.

His Roman adversaries, however, pursued him. In the year 1731, their violence against the family of Rajanaiken resulted in the death of his father. A number of armed Roman Catholics attacked him and his relations under pretext of a quarrel about some property, and while the old man was trying to defend his youngest son from the murderers, he was himself overpowered. Rajanaiken fled from the house naked, but while he was being pursued the military rescued him. In the year 1732, they sent assassins to his house by night to murder him, but the attempt failed. The year after, he and his companions were attacked by ruffians set up by his enemies on the road to Tranquebar. One of them drew a sword and was about to smite him when his wife threw herself between him and the assailant and he was able to escape. This kind of thing happened almost every year, but he bore all these troubles with exemplary patience. 'As I have to bear so much contempt, abuse and threatening,' he writes in 1735, ' I will tell you how I console myself. The Lord means well towards me both for time and for eternity; the sufferings which he sends me will work for me a far more exceeding weight of glory, for which I look with anxious trust. I have not been able to hide these thoughts from my people. God has graciously granted me this relief, and without His will nothing can happen to me.' His patience and long-suffering were blessed, for he won many souls, amongst them some of his most violent enemies. His experience in the army made it possible for him to convert several soldiers to the new faith. He possessed a thorough knowledge of the Bible, and in spite of his poor education was a fluent and forceful speaker.

About this time the health of Pastor Aaron was failing, owing to age and his severe exertions in visiting the village congregations. The missionaries therefore wrote home for permission to ordain another ' country priest'. Friends in Europe who had heard of the character and abilities of Rajanaiken considered him the most suitable person for ordination. His work had been such an outstanding success and so greatly blessed by God and he himself had been so steadfast under the severest persecution that there could have been no better choice. But the hydra-headed monster of caste showed its head. Rajanaiken was of a low caste—an untouchable. The missionaries thus described in a letter to the Principal at Halle the difficulty which this created. ' Not you only, but several of us, desired to ordain Rajanaiken to the office of priest. This might be done if he were to confine his labour to the pariahs. It is true there are several very honest and respectable persons among them, like Rajanaiken himself; still, from the general low character of those people, the Christians of higher caste avoid coming in contact with any of them. We take great pains to lessen these prejudices among our Christians : still to a certain degree they must be taken into consideration. Rajanaiken is very useful and successful in his labour as a catechist in his four districts. But we should greatly hesitate to have the Lord's supper administered by him, lest it should diminish the regard of Christians of higher caste for that sacrament itself.' They thought that his having been born an untouchable was an insuperable obstacle to his becoming a priest. Instead of facing it boldly, they preferred to ordain the Tranquebar catechist, Diogo. The ordination took place on December the 28th, 1741 : and Diogo was sent to Tanjore and placed in charge of all the districts to the south.

This by no means discouraged Rajanaiken who had himself never sought for any preferment. A letter which he wrote to Professor Franck of Halle on the 4th of January 1743 fully reveals his real humility and sincerity : ' It seems wonderful indeed that God should have chosen me as an instrument to spread His word among the heathen, and to make me an assistant to the missionaries sent from your country. I am not worthy to bear such an office. Still, since God has thought fit to make use of me, I often times pray to Him, " What Thou wilt have done through my feeble powers, O Lord, enable me to do ! " I pray also to be delivered from all that is earthly within me. I have five under-catechists to assist me, whom I often examine, exhort and instruct, to prepare them for their duties in their several districts. I preach the Gospel to the heathen: and those who have already embraced Christianity I strengthen, warn and encourage. I salute all that have shown me so much kindness. To Christ who has appeared in the flesh, the Almighty Father and the blessed Spirit be praise and honour and glory for ever and ever. Amen.'

It seems to us inexcusable that such a man should not have been ordained merely because of his humble origin. The poison of caste is the 'strongest foe to the Gospel of Christ', especially in South India. It has bound the people body and soul, 'in a bondage perfectly incomprehensible to the western mind'.

The Church at Tanjore suffered much during the siege of the French in 1758. Rajanaiken himself refused to flee from the town. A Captain Berg in the Raja's service, however, gave the Christians much help and offered Rajanaiken a house near the garrison of the Indian troops on condition that he would assemble those who were willing for prayers morning and evening. Rajanaiken was then beginning to feel the infirmities of age and his health was failing, but he gladly acceded to the proposal. At first, the soldiers seemed to dislike the service, but after a time, pleased with Rajanaiken, they cheerfully joined in his prayers.

In the year 1772 he died, after forty-four years of labour and suffering in the Saviour's cause. The end came suddenly, after he had been preaching to his flock. He is a striking example of the power of God and of His ability to use as His instruments the weaklings of the earth. His life shows what can be accomplished by workers even of the lowest caste if they are utterly devoted to God, and how, when the word of God is preached in the power of the Holy Spirit accompanied by faithful living, it is as 'quick and powerful' from the lips of illiterate low-born men as when spoken by the learned and eloquent.

The sequel is also remarkable. The missionaries were unable to find a suitable successor to Rajanaiken. His widow, a woman of genuine piety and a sincere Christian, who had long taken an active though unobtrusive part in her husband's work, was appointed. She employed herself principally in teaching the catechism to enquirers and thus carried on her husband's noble work for some time.

II. AARON

The first 'country-priest'

In any list of the heroes of the Indian Church the name of Aaron, the first Indian Christian minister of the Protestant Church, must be mentioned. That within twenty-seven years of the arrival of the first Protestant missionaries there had been found one worthy to be ordained as a minister shows not only that the foundations were from the very outset firm and that the converts were properly trained towards an unshakable faith, but also that even the uneducated rural people of India, if given education and adequately taught the rudiments of the Christian faith, can become leaders in the Church—a fact which has been sufficiently demonstrated in the subsequent history of the Indian Church.

Aaron was born of Hindu parents at Cuddalore about the year 1698. His father, Chokkanathapillai, was a merchant in fairly affluent circumstances and of a very respectable caste. He had his son taught to read and write and instructed in the Hindu religion. It happened that the charity school for Indian children founded by the English in 1717 in Cuddalore was exactly opposite to his father's house, so that he made acquaintance with the catechist in charge of it, and from him obtained some biblical books and read them diligently. They made a strong impression on him. 'The word of God worked like a fire within me,' as he says in one of his letters. The wise providence of God when He chooses His servants is further seen in that his father got into trouble with the Company, lost all his wealth and was obliged to leave Cuddalore, and eventually became too poor to support him. Then what he had heard of Christianity came to his mind and he went to Tranquebar where he hoped to be taken care of. On arrival he went straight to the catechist Savarimuthu from Cuddalore, who received him kindly and took him to Ziegenbalg, who placed him under instruction and finally baptized him in the year 1718. His parents, on hearing this, wished to take him away, but he refused to go. He was first employed as a schoolmaster, but was soon made a catechist. His faithfulness and superior abilities won for him the full confidence of the missionaries, of whom he became a trusted colleague. He was not able to convert his father, but had the joy of seeing his mother and sisters accept the Christian faith.

The work of the missionaries was so successful and the number of Christian congregations had increased so much in number and were scattered in so many villages that the need for visiting them frequently and for administering the sacraments was being increasingly felt. It was not possible for the missionaries to do all this visiting themselves. The obvious solution was to ordain an Indian priest for the village congregations. Being only presbyters themselves, they did not consider themselves at liberty to take such an important step without seeking advice from their superiors in Denmark. In the year 1728 they wrote to Copenhagen asking for authority from the Mission College and the concurrence of the King of Denmark to ordain an Indian priest. They wrote, 'Our great desire now is to provide the congregations which have risen up in the interior with the proper means for the care of their souls. It is not so easy to go ourselves into the country to help these people. They are obliged to come to us, especially when they need the holy sacraments, but there are great difficulties in the way of this and in some cases it is quite impossible. The best solution to all these difficulties would be to ordain a minister for these people from among themselves if one could be found with suitable qualities. Therefore we wish to ask the College how far our power would extend in such a case.'

The reply was what was only to be expected: 'The good hope which you express of finding natives who may in time become teachers and shepherds of their country people has rejoiced us much. With the most gracious permission of His Majesty, we therefore give you power to ordain in the name of the Lord a person of Indian origin who shall be suitable for

the work of the ministry and to confide one or more districts
to his care.'

The permission sought for and thus received was not acted
upon hurriedly. The missionaries waited for nearly five years
before giving effect to it, as they realized the supreme importance of the step they were about to take, and waited on God for
clear guidance. In the spring of 1733, however, they decided
to ordain one among their three senior catechists—Savarimuthu, Diogo and Aaron—and set about prayerfully preparing
them for ordination, giving them daily instruction in pastoral
theology. It is somewhat surprising but gratifying that they
wanted to leave to the congregation the final choice. An
assembly of the congregation was held on the 25th of March to
inform them that they should make the choice, and to exhort
them to place the matter individually before God in prayer in
order that they might be helped to choose wisely. Savarimuthu
begged to be excused from the great responsibility, so that the
choice lay between Aaron and Diogo. Those two preached
their trial sermons about Whitsuntide; and on the 27th of
May, the heads of families were called into the church and
after prayer each one was asked to go into the vestry and record
his vote. It so happened that there was an equal number of
votes for each of the candidates. The missionaries also were
equally divided, three for Aaron and three for Diogo. They
therefore let the matter rest for some months. Later in the year,
however, Aaron, the older of the two, proved to be the unani-
mous choice of the people. He was thereupon ordained on the
28th of December 1733, in the presence of a large congregation
of European and Indian Christians, eleven clergyman being
present and participating in the laying on of hands—the six
missionaries of the place, Sartorius from Madras, the two
Danish ministers of Tranquebar, and two ship chaplains. The
service of ordination was performed in Tamil according to the
rites of the Lutheran Church. After this the newly made priest
delivered a sermon on Galatians 4.4-5: 'When the fulness
of time was come, God sent forth His Son, made of a woman,
made under the law, to redeem them that were under the law,
that we might receive the adoption of sons.' His exposition

of the verse showed that he was fully fitted for the office to which he had been called. Sartorius, while writing about it, said, ' He preached with great cheerfulness and particularly exhorted the Christians from the country who were to be his special charge to be thankful for the benefits that would thus be bestowed on them, while he begged others to pray God to give him the gifts necessary for his office. By constant journeys into the country he has gained great practice and according to the testimony of all who know him he has hitherto proved himself very faithful. He has very dignified and agreeable manners which gifts of nature are rare amongst the Malabarians.' Aaron was then about thirty-five years of age.

The news of his ordination—the first Indian to become a priest—thrilled people in England, Germany and Denmark, who were inspired to greater hopes regarding the evangelization of India. The high-caste Hindus now treated him with even greater respect. They knew what dignity attached itself to the priestly office. The Christians were particularly gratified that one of their own number should have been raised to such a dignity.

After his ordination the missionaries kept him for some time in Tranquebar in order that he might be helped in the discharge of his new duties by their advice. After a time they placed him in charge of a district which contained Christians in no less than fifty-six towns and villages. He moved about among these scattered congregations, performing divine service on the Lord's Day alternately at the four principal stations and visiting the villages during the week. At the great festivals of the Church the villages were assembled at central places where he celebrated the Lord's Supper. He so arranged that in the course of the year all had an opportunity to partake of it. It was soon manifest that the Lord's blessing rested upon his labours. As early as the month of January 1734, fifty converts were added to the Church as the fruit of the seed he had sown.

An abstract from Aaron's own account of his journeyings throws light on the continuous zeal with which he worked. It is an account of a journey in March 1734. He and his companion set out into the country. To the first Hindu he meets he preaches about the true worship of God, which angers him so much that he orders them all out of his house. The little band, driven out of the village itself, takes a meal on the banks of a river. Next day, they meet a small congregation living with difficulty in the midst of non-Christians. An old woman has a curious request, 'As I am getting old, ask your assistant catechist to take better care of my soul,' she says to Aaron. The next day he meets and talks to forty-two people in a house, of whom two promise to follow Christ. The following day he meets a man who does not know how to pray. Aaron writes out on a palm-leaf a small prayer and teaches him about worship. And so on, he goes from village to village, untiring and restless. He is not hasty in baptizing people, he does not jump to conclusions as soon as anyone expresses some interest. We read of a sick man he meets on this journey who asked for baptism. Aaron had been putting it off 'in order to awaken a deeper reverence and a more ardent desire for the holy ordinance in his soul.' And while on his sick-bed a conversation ensues, at the end of which Aaron finally tests his belief and baptizes him.

He continued thus year after year, occupied almost constantly with journeys to the villages in his charge. In order to relieve him of part of the fatigue, a horse was procured. Yet his health suffered much. He lived on the best terms with all his colleagues, and especially with Diogo, who shared his work. Both were humble spirits. 'I am like a child compared to Diogo,' Aaron once said, 'with regard to knowledge and ability.' Diogo always said that Aaron could manage the people much better than he could. The reports of the missionaries to Denmark at this time were full of the excellent work which Aaron was doing. 'He preaches the word of God at various places, superintends the carrying out of proper discipline and order, manages and encourages the catechists, in which things he has made great progress. May God preserve his delicate health in these journeys which on account of the heat, the wind, the dust and the wading through water, are very arduous in this country.'

This was very true for Aaron was in poor health and the long journeys were becoming too much for him. But he would not give up. In one of his last two letters to the mission in Europe, he wrote, 'Though my bodily weakness is a great hindrance to my journeys, I wish to work as much as possible for the benefit of souls. . . . I will patiently bear all crosses and trials that may come upon me for the sake of Christ.'

With this determination Aaron carried on till 1745, when he was able to continue his journeys only in much suffering. But he did not relax in his work, though thoughts of death hovered over him. When he was told of the sudden death of one of his acquaintances, he said, 'If that strong and healthy man is dead, how much ought I to think of it.' In all his journeys that year he acted as if it were to be his last and always bade farewell to the missionaries and other friends as if he should never see them again. His last journey was in the month of June, when he set out to celebrate the feast of Whitsun-tide in Mayavaram district. All the Christians around were assembled at Thattanur and Aaron preached to them impress-ively, though he seemed to be in great pain. He told them that it was the last time he would celebrate the feast among them and that therefore they must observe it properly and see that it became a blessing to them and not a curse. He returned home very ill and said to a missionary who came to see him, 'My country journeys are ended.' He came to Tranquebar at the end of June to see his daughter married to the son of Diogo on the 23rd, and the next day became seriously ill and was in much agony, though fully conscious and completely resting his hope on his Lord. In the afternoon he received the Eucharist in the presence of priest Diogo and many Christians and died on the 25th of June (1745) aged forty-seven, after twenty-four years of hard work and severe suffering and eleven years in the pastoral office. He was buried in the Old Jerusalem Church.

The first Indian ordained minister of the Church had fully justified the wisdom of the step that had been taken. He had not only rendered faithful service but had conducted himself in such a way that men of all faiths 'not only respected him, but loved and trusted him'. In times of difficulty in congregations his advice was valued, coming from his upright judgment and his experience. As a pastor he had intimate knowledge of the needs of all members of a congregation, could tell what was wanting in each and how he should be guided. Another unique characteristic of his was that he possessed a peculiar ability for learning, even from very simple people, in what way God had first drawn their souls to Himself. He warned and punished evildoers earnestly and impressively, but the sick and the suffering he treated with love. He bore his sufferings with extraordinary courage and firmness. The first Indian clergyman was a noble example for all who followed him in the sacred office.

III. SATHYANADHAN

The first Indian 'Superintending Missionary'

Mention has already been made of Sathyanadhan, the first ordained minister of the Church in Tinnevelly, first in the line of 'country priests' in Tinnevelly as regards character as well as in the order of time—a man of true Christian integrity, fearlessness and earnestness.

The reason for the presence of Protestant Christians in the Tinnevelly district, which had long been the scene of Roman Catholic missionary activity, is obscure. Apparently the earliest Christians came from Trichinopoly and Tanjore, fleeing from those places during the disturbances caused by the war with the French. The establishment by the East India Company of a military garrison in Palamcottah in 1765 must also have had something to do with it. When C. F. Schwartz, the famous missionary of Tanjore, visited Palamcottah in the year 1780, he found there a small congregation numbering forty persons of whom the most prominent was a Brahmin widow who had been living with a British military officer, by whom she had been taught the rudiments of Christianity. Schwartz baptized her with the name Clorinda. She built at her own expense a small chapel which was consecrated by him in 1785. There was, however, no one to minister to this small, isolated group of Christians so far away from centres of Christian activity. In 1783, two converts went to Tanjore and begged Schwartz to send them a pastor. Thereupon, in January 1785, he sent a much valued catechist, by name Sathyanadhan, to Palamcottah and himself followed and spent three months in the district. He found small isolated groups of Christians in several places round about and signs of a religious unrest which indicated the working of the Spirit of God among the people; and he prophesied that Tinnevelly would be the scene of a great harvest for God. He returned to Tanjore, leaving Sathyanadhan in charge of the whole work in that district.

Very little, however, is known about the early life of Sathyanadhan. He was a Hindu of Tanjore, converted to Christianity after he had grown into manhood. He was brought to Schwartz in the year 1772 by one of the catechists who met him in the country. Remaining at Trichinopoly several days, he heard in silence the instructions given there and at length avowed his conviction of the falsehood of heathenism. He continued to attend diligently to reading and prayer and gave such proofs of sincerity that he was baptized, receiving the name of Sathyanadhan (Possessor of Truth). He came of a high caste and Schwartz entertained great hopes of him, which were later fulfilled beyond his expectations. He was so zealous, sincere and capable in spite of his lack of good education that Schwartz appointed him as catechist to a place called Vallam, seven miles from Tanjore, where he gave such a good account of himself that he became one of Schwartz's trusted assistants. Later, when a reliable person was needed for the work in Tinnevelly, he was selected.

After Sathyanadhan went to Tinnevelly the work progressed rapidly. The congregations were visited only once a year by some ordained minister from Tranquebar or Tanjore who administered the Sacraments. By the year 1786, a congregation of about a hundred and sixty persons had been gathered, and the need for an ordained man was increasingly felt. In August 1790 Schwartz decided to ordain Sathyanadhan, and called him to Tanjore in order to prepare him. On the 26th of December 1790 he was ordained according to the rules of the Lutheran Church, and preached a powerful sermon in Tamil, which was translated into English, sent to England and published in the report of the Society for the Promotion of Christian Knowledge for the year 1792. The Society remarked that the sermon showed the capacity of the people of India for the office of the ministry and that the efforts of the missionaries to train them for the work had not been in vain. Immediately after his ordination Sathyanadhan returned to Palamcottah and resumed his work. Referring to his ordination, M. Kohlhoff gave this testimony, ' God had blessed the labours of this worthy man in awakening many to turn from their sins to God : and no doubts were entertained but he would prove a blessed instrument in the hands of the Almighty for the enlargement of His Kingdom upon earth.'

In the year 1792, he was greatly encouraged by a letter from the S.P.C.K., confirming him in his appointment and exhorting him to continue his labours in the Lord's vineyard as faithfully as he had done in the past. Sathyanadhan sent a reply to this letter in which he said, ' Whoever knows the Truth and the design for which it was revealed and enjoys the blessings of our holy religion, he and he only is fit to recommend it to others. One who does not live up to the design of it and does not lead a holy life, though he should speak as an angel from heaven, yet his life not being correspondent with his doctrine, his preaching will often be in vain. That this may not be the case with me, I shall always endeavour to be watchful.'

Sathyanadhan was in sole charge of the work in Tinnevelly and adjoining districts for six years, no European missionary having been sent after Jænicke left it owing to illness. It was during that period that a movement began among one of the more numerous Hindu communities in the district—the Shanars—which in course of time became a mass movement. The new converts, however, did not have unworthy motives in becoming Christians; in fact, they suffered materially by so doing. They did not receive any financial help from the

Mission which was itself very poor, but were severely persecuted by their Hindu neighbours. No amount of persecution,
however, was able to quench the flame which had begun to
spread all over the area. Accessions to the Church went on
increasing in number, and not a single case of apostasy was
reported.

In the year 1805, Sathyanadhan, finding it difficult to get
on with the local people who considered him an outsider—he
being a native of Tanjore—and did not treat him well, returned
to Tanjore at his own request.

When Dr. Claudius Buchanan visited Tanjore in 1806 he
found Sathyanadhan 'advanced in years, his black locks
grown grey'. He heard him preach at the service in Tamil
and was greatly impressed. It was obvious that the sermon on
'The Marvellous Light' had a perceptible effect on the hearers.
Sathyanadhan described the pagan darkness, then the light of
Ziegenbalg, the light of Schwartz and finally the heavenly
light, when there shall be no more need of the light of the sun
or the moon.

Sathyanadhan, who passed away at Tanjore in 1815, was one
of that group of early pioneers to whom the Church, especially
in Tinnevelly, should be everlastingly grateful. He worked
without sparing himself and with no thought of any reward
except the joy of seeing souls gathered into the true faith. But
for him there might not have been so large a Church in Tinnevelly to-day. He nursed it through all its early troubles
and left it firmly established, equipped with churches and
catechists.

Schwartz said about him, 'His humble, disinterested and
believing work has been made so evident to me and to others
that I may say with truth I have never met his equal among
the natives of this country. His gift in preaching affords universal satisfaction. His love to the poor is extraordinary and it
is often inconceivable to me how he can manage to subsist
on his scanty stipend and yet do so much in relieving the
poor.'

He demonstrated very early in the life of the Church in
India that Indians are capable of leadership, can be trusted

with responsibility and can carry on the work of evangelization and superintendence as effectively as any European missionary—a position which has not yet been universally
accepted.

IV. Abdul Maseeh

Abdul Maseeh, the first Indian Mohammedan to be admitted
to holy orders in the Church of England in India, must receive
honourable place in any list of its heroes. It has always been
very difficult to convince Mohammedans of the truth of
Christianity, because they consider their religion a later and
more perfect revelation. Their religious fervour and their
social solidarity form almost insuperable obstacles to their
acceptance of Christian truth. But in those early days the
difficulties were a hundred-fold greater. And when the truth
was accepted in the face of such great odds it meant no small
strength of conviction and no mean courage. Besides this,
Abdul Maseeh's conversion offers yet one more illustration of
the truth that ' the word of God is sharper than any two-edged
sword ' and when placed in the hands of anyone who takes
the trouble to read it can lead him to the way of salvation.

Sheikh Salih, the future Abdul Maseeh, was born in a respectable and orthodox Mohammedan family at Delhi. His
father, a zealous Mohammedan, taught him religion and im-
parted to him a thorough knowledge of Persian and Arabic.
At twenty-one he became a *munshee* (private language tutor)
first to an English merchant and then to an officer in the
Company's service. At that time he was exceedingly zealous
for the faith of Islam and induced a Hindu servant of his
employer to become a Muslim. On his master reproving him
for this, he became offended and left his employ with a determination to have nothing more to do with the English. After
this he engaged himself in a variety of pursuits and visited
different parts of the country. Finally, he went to Cawnpore
to visit his father who was then a private tutor in a wealthy
family. Their house happened to be close to Mr. Martyn's

premises. The Rev. Henry Martyn was then the chaplain of Cawnpore, but was an ardent evangelist, holding frequent public disputations and discussions with the *mullahs*, the learned men of Islam. Being zealous, Sheikh Salih once went to see Henry Martyn baited in the controversy, but Martyn's words in exposition of the ten commandments and his arguments in proof of Christianity sank into his heart. He had not been quite satisfied and was perplexed about the contradictions maintained by the different Mohammedan sects, and this Christian instruction appeared to him better than any he had received. He mentioned this to his father and begged him to get him some employment in Cawnpore so that he could hear more about these things. Through the influence of a friend, Sheikh Salih was engaged, in May 1810, to copy Persian writings for Sabat, who was then helping Martyn to translate the New Testament into Hindustani. He obtained lodgings on the premises and thus had many opportunities of learning more about Christian truth. In his eagerness to know more about Christianity he used to enquire from the Christian children in Martyn's school about the lessons they were taught.

When Martyn had finished his translation of the New Testament the book was given to Sheikh Salih to bind. He seized the opportunity to study it and soon perceived the truth and decided in favour of the Christian religion, but did not reveal it to anyone, till Martyn was about to leave Cawnpore. He then opened his mind to him and asked for advice. But Martyn was not convinced that Sheikh Salih was fit to be baptized and took him along in October 1810 to Calcutta, having decided for reasons of health to leave India and return to England via Persia. He left him with Mr. Brown and went away in January 1811. After five months' further delay, Mr. Brown, being satisfied with his conduct, baptized him on Whitsunday in the Old Church, with the Christian name Abdul Maseeh— the Servant of Christ.

After his baptism Abdul Maseeh continued to live in Calcutta where he made himself very useful especially in preaching to non-Christians; but he was, however, subject to much vexation from the Mohammedans of the place. After a short while the Rev. Daniel Corrie, who was about to proceed to Agra as chaplain, took him under his protection. They left Calcutta for Agra on the 20th of November 1812, and reached Agra on March the 18th, 1813. On the 22nd they opened a school, where they taught the Church catechism in the mornings, and Persian during the day. They also carried on conversations and discussions with respectable and scholarly Mohammedans, but with little immediate result. But, as time went on, there were several, mostly Hindus, whose hearts were changed and who were baptized. The progress of the Gospel created a general stir in the place and a Mohammedan *moulvi* (judge) used his influence to persecute the converts. The conduct of the new Christians, however, made an impression on their neighbours, who said, 'People do become inoffensive when they become Christians.' One after another was added to the Church until on Christmas Day 1813 twenty adults and twelve children were baptized and there were forty-five communicants. Corrie and Abdul had learned the need for great caution in admitting candidates to baptism. No one was received without an open profession of readiness to bear the Cross.

The next year, Corrie left for England, placing Abdul in charge of the congregation in Agra. Having studied some medical books during an illness and acquired some knowledge of simple medicine, he began to use this successfully in the service of God. He wrote to Corrie, 'I give medicine and food at my own charge to the poor, and have collected nearly fifty books on medicine. From the time I commenced this plan, three hundred people, by the favour of God, have received help in different diseases. God often, by this means, makes some of this city who were enemies to become friends. Many of the poor of the city come and, taking occasion from their bodily complaints, I try to heal their souls. May the Holy Spirit so shed down His grace that like as many attend for bodily healing they may assemble for spiritual healing.'

In the autumn of 1820, Abdul had received Lutheran orders at Calcutta, Bishop Middleton finding that he had no powers to ordain an Indian. Bishop Heber, his successor, however, felt differently. It was also deemed advisable that as a missionary of the Church of England, Abdul Maseeh should receive epis-copal ordination. So, on November the 30th, 1825, he was ordained along with two European missionaries of the C.M.S. in the Calcutta Cathedral. 'This excited a strong sensation among the natives as he was the first Mussulman who became a minister of the Gospel. It gave him, however, a certain standing and influence over his countrymen. On his way up from Calcutta to Agra he was treated everywhere with the most marked respect and on Easter Sunday of that year he adminis-tered the Eucharist in the Urdu language to Europeans, native Christians, Romanists and Armenians.'

But Abdul did not live long to labour as a clergyman of the Church of England. After his ordination he set out for Luck-now, where his mother resided, and reached there during the hot weather of 1826. It was intended that he should make this place the sphere of his future labours; but on the 4th of March 1827 he was called to his eternal rest. According to his desire, his remains were interred in the compound of his own house and the Resident at Lucknow attended the funeral and read the funeral service at the grave. A monument was also erected over the grave under his orders with a suitable inscrip-tion in both English and Persian.

In the report of the Calcutta Committee for 1827 the follow-ing notice of his work appeared: 'He had laboured in the service of the Church Missionary Society upward of fourteen years, during the whole of which period he had uniformly adorned the doctrine of God our Saviour, and greatly en-deared himself to many Christians of all classes in society. By patience and meekness under persecutions and reproaches for Christ's sake, and by persevering endeavours to return good for evil, even his enemies had become at peace with him; while, by his labours to make known the Gospel, multitudes of his countrymen were brought to acknowledge the superiority of the Christian religion, and about a hundred of them to embrace the profession of it. Many of these departed this life before him, some have returned to their old errors, and some remain walking in the truth. While the Committee justly regret the loss which the cause of the Gospel has suffered in the removal of so valuable a fellow-labourer, they would offer their hearty thanks to the Father of Light, from whom every good and perfect gift doth come, for manifesting so signally the power of his grace in the conversion, holy life, and triumphant death of this true servant of Christ.'

VII

THE ACHIEVEMENTS OF
THE CHRISTIAN MOVEMENT IN INDIA

WHAT then is the result of all the activities summarized in the foregoing pages? Has the presence of Christians in the country for more than two hundred years meant anything to its people? Has the nation at large been affected in any way by the presence of a community of people who forsook their ancestral faith and followed the religion of the foreigner? Has the coming of Christianity from the west been of any significance to India?

As has been seen, the coming of Christianity to India was undoubtedly providential—clearly part of God's plans for the country. Had it not been for this political and religious contact with the nations of the west and predominantly with one of them, it is quite possible that India would still have been as she had been for ages. The foreign invader and the Christian missionary are together responsible for all the changes of the last two hundred years. If to-day we rejoice in our independence, in our democracy, in the influential place which we occupy in the councils of the world, in our leadership in East Asia—we owe our present position of worth and influence not a little to our impact with the west, to the moral, spiritual and cultural elements which we have imbibed from our western mentors and instructors, to the ideas of freedom and self-determination which were generated by our study and appreciation of the literatures of the west and more than a little to the training and grounding in administration which we got during our apprenticeship under British supervision. Our democratic institutions, our administrative machinery, our parliamentary system, the very language we use all come from the west and are the products of our intimate contact with Christian Britain during the last two hundred years. It is difficult to distinguish between these two streams of influence —the political and the religious—and assess their respective results. Western civilization is a chemical compound of which the main element is the Christian tradition. The results of the impact of western civilization and the western way of life on the Indian people were therefore, very naturally, both political and religious.

The creation and consolidation of a Christian community is perhaps the least of the effects of this impact. At the moment there are about nine million people professing the new faith, forming two per cent of the total population and the second largest minority community in it. There were in the year 1941, according to the census taken then, 4,572,339 non-Roman Christians and 4,317,067 Roman Catholic Christians in India (now India and Pakistan). The number must, of course, have increased since. In literacy the Indian Christian community has advanced far beyond the general population. The percentage of literates in the Christian community is as high as ninety in the United States of Travancore and Cochin, 38·5 in the Central Provinces and 25 on an average throughout the country. The average for the whole population was only 12·2 per cent in 1941.

Eighty years ago a speaker at a missionary conference in South India said, ' Native society generally is becoming conscious of the existence of this new growth (the Indian Church) in their midst. Its blade is piercing at not a few points the hard crust of Indian soil, its vitality is undoubted, and feeble as it still may be, there is an impression abroad that it is destined to become a mighty growth overshadowing the whole land.' It may not be that it has yet become ' a mighty growth overshadowing the whole land ', but it has become a virile young tree and his rapidly growing larger and mightier.

The magnitude of this achievement can be best appreciated

only if we bear in mind the conditions under which this community came into being. Long years had to be spent preparing the way for it and this preparation had to be made in the midst of many unfavourable circumstances.

For several decades after the commencement of missionary activity, work was largely preparatory in nature, consisting principally of the collection of materials for future use and experimentation with methods. It is obvious that when trying to evangelize a vast country like India, ' with an immense population speaking many languages, and possessing an elaborate and ancient system of religion, defended by an intelligent and learned hierarchy, and sustained by complicated ceremonials and rituals, and by manifold sensuous representations ', a long, costly and wide-based preparation is necessary. The translation of the Christian Scriptures into the several languages, the preparation of material for the initial instruction of catechumens and beginners in the faith, the production of apologetic booklets, tracts and handbills to be placed in the hands of those who come to listen to the preaching of the word, the establishment of schools and colleges, the erection of churches and school buildings, the provision of institutions where the new converts may be trained for employment either within or outside the Church—all these take a long time, great labour and the expenditure of much money and energy. That is why in every mission the first few years produced no appreciable results. The accession of large numbers came later when the materials thus laboriously amassed could be fully employed and more aggressive work begun.

The next factor which constituted, during the earliest years of the movement, a handicap to the rapid formation of a new Indian Christian community was the opposition by the Government of the day, which was firm in its conviction that it was wiser not to touch the religion and civilization of India: and it was the prevailing opinion among the officials of Government that it was impossible to induce Hindus and Muslims to change either their religion or their social practices. They thought so highly of Indian religious thought that it seemed impertinent to attempt to modify it in any way. They were afraid that any attempt to tamper with the religious belief of the people would endanger their trade and administration.

Such fears were unfounded and proved false by subsequent events. When, for example, it was decided by Parliament that the whole of India (and Australia) was to be constituted into a Bishopric and that the Bishop should have Calcutta as his headquarters, the East India Company thought that this decision and the coming of the Bishop should be kept a secret from the people of India lest the Hindus and Muslims should be alarmed at the coming of a high dignitary of the Church and be afraid that a powerful assault was to be made on their religious systems. But as Sir John Kaye points out somewhat sarcastically, 'There was no excitement. Offended Hinduism did not rise up in arms, nor indignant Mohammedanism raise a war-cry of death to the infidel. The Bishop preached in the Christian temple, and that night the Europeans slept soundly in their beds. There was not a massacre; there was not a rebellion. It really seemed probable, after all, that British dominion in the East would survive the blow.'

But such an unsympathetic and discouraging attitude towards Christian work in the country constituted a severe handicap to it and, coupled with the un-Christian lives of the European laity, considerably retarded the progress of the Gospel.

And when we remember also the opposition from the Hindu religious organization itself, the social ostracism of the new convert which has been the rule from the beginning and is even now almost universal, the fact that, however deep may be the religious conviction which prompted his change of religion, the new convert does still find it impossible entirely to cut himself away from his old social and religious moorings, that the strongest temptations are offered to him by his neighbours and relatives to renounce his new faith and that physical violence, threats, persecution and persuasion are all employed in trying to wean him from his new allegiance—then only do we realize what a great achievement is the creation of a

Christian community of this size and worth in this country. 'This is the Lord's doing: and it is marvellous in our eyes.'

The strength and the results of the Christian movement in India cannot, however, be measured merely by the number of professed Christians, or even by the cultural, intellectual and spiritual attainments of the leaders and the general level of the masses of the new community. The indirect influence of Christianity is as remarkable and worthy of note as the baptism of converts and the formation of Christian groups throughout the land. The great progress in the enlightenment of the people, the general awakening of thought throughout the country, the wonderful transformation which Indian society has undergone, the almost universal yearning after something better than a religion with its myriads of gods can give, the desire for a holier and purer faith—all these are due to the spread of Christian principles which are enlarging the minds, stimulating the conscience and quickening the religious sense of the Hindus. The moral growth of the nation and the radical changes taking place in Indian society are as much evidences of the progress of the Christian religion as the conversion of some to the faith. The Christian movement has been a spiritual ferment and stimulus to Hindu society. Its influence has permeated the life, thinking and social action of Hindus and has introduced into them a new set of ethical values. It was Christianity which awakened the conscience of Hindu society in respect of the millions of outcastes and inaugurated the movement which recently culminated in the removal of untouchability by the new Constitution of India. It was with the gradual permeation of Christian ideas that a new reverence for womanhood came to be, till, at the moment, both in the eyes of the law and in social convention, all disabilities under which Indian women have been suffering for untold ages have been removed. To-day a woman can be the Governor of a province, the Minister of a state or a member of the state legislatures. Women can and have become leaders in public life. The idea of home life of a type very different from the ancient Hindu model is also directly the creation of Christian ideas. The new respect for human personality, the present eagerness to

deal fairly with workers and the lower classes in general is also
to be attributed to conceptions borrowed from Christianity,
which has done more for the elevation of Indian society in the
one century than its predecessors did in all the ages of their respective dominion.

A further effect of the Christian impact on the Hindu religion
may be seen in the present intellectual and moral condition
of the followers of that religion. Those in the villages who are
still illiterate have not in the least changed so far as their
beliefs and practices are concerned; but the educated Hindu
has for the most part been profoundly affected by Christianity
and the education he has received, perhaps in a Christian school
or college. While there are quite a few whose moral nature is
entirely unaffected and who have not been touched in their
beliefs in spite of contact with Christianity and in spite of their
education, and who are as thorough-going and orthodox
Hindus as their forefathers, a very large number have completely lost their faith in popular idolatry, have no use for the
priestly class and have given up performing the numerous
ceremonies prescribed by orthodoxy. Some of them, however,
take up an orthodox position from intellectual sensitiveness.
They do not like to despise a religion that has flourished in
the country for three thousand years and whose philosophy has
captivated many western minds. But a large section are fast
drifting into scepticism or gross indifference to spiritual things.
They have found their own religion wholly dissatisfying and
have concluded that all religions are very much alike. Their
minds have been swept clean by higher education, but no sub-
stitute for their old beliefs has been put in. Their minds are
awake, their moral natures quickened, their mental attitudes
largely moulded by western thought and feeling and their
reasoning faculty brightly cultivated, but conscience and will
are comparatively untrained. Once they enter life they completely lose all that they have gained and drift into complete
indifference to religion. They smother their higher instincts
and aspirations by engrossing themselves in politics. What
has been said of the educated classes of ancient Rome may be
said of them: 'They outwardly conform to the rites which they

inwardly despise.' Quite a few of them do not make even this pretence of being Hindus. They have no serious religious principle or desire or thought, and are given up to worldliness and practical godlessness. Their lives are characterized by a superficial rationalism which tends to demoralize the individual and discredit the community, though outwardly they conform to Hindu customs and ceremonies, chiefly on social grounds.

So far as their attitude to Christianity is concerned there is an increasing disposition to separate the morality and history of the gospel from its theological aspect; in other words, to distinguish between Christ and Christianity. Not infrequently Christ's divine nature is granted; but He is but one emanation from the divine—one among several others. All admit that against Him nothing can be said. There is a very real admiration of His character, but they feel no call to accept His teaching and example and the way of salvation which He has revealed. Often they question the claims of Christianity on the ground that the popular faith is not altogether the system which Christ founded and that the lives of His followers are inconsistent with their profession. There is also a complete absence of a sense of personal responsibility. While they disapprove of many things in their own religion and in their society, they do not think it is their duty to remedy those evils. A moral inability to see any necessary connection between faith and practice is characteristic of the Hindu attitude of mind at the present time. The greatest need is to quicken the sense of individual responsibility and of the terrible nature of sin.

That the Indian Christian community is well in advance of other communities in education and literacy is well known. It contains also a larger percentage of persons literate in English. In female education they outdistance the other communities, except perhaps the Parsis, by a very long lead. In general literacy and literacy in English, Indian Christian women are far ahead of any other community, the proportion per 1,000 being 29 for Indian Christian women, 1·4 for Hindus and ·9 for Muslims. This spread of education among Indian

Christians has been a great advantage to the nation. Seven per cent of those engaged in the teaching profession are Indian Christians and one can distinctly recall the time when a hundred per cent of the women employed as school-teachers were Indian Christians; and among Indian women doctors there were till even a few years ago no representatives of any other community but the Indian Christian. The service the community has rendered to the nation as teachers of the young, as doctors and nurses, midwives and health workers in villages has been of inestimable value: though its uniqueness and distinctiveness has, of course, been lost in recent years. The community has also rendered distinct service to the nation by giving to the public services and to the learned professions a large number of individuals whose work has been of outstanding merit. The Indian Christian's freedom from communal prejudice, his general uprightness of character, his ability to hold the scales even between other communities, are well known and used to be taken advantage of in the administration.

Similarly, the community has also contributed outstanding leaders to public life. From the very earliest days there has been a stream of distinguished, highly educated Indian Christian men and women whose intellectual and moral pre-eminence was readily accepted by the whole community. The Indian Christian community has produced poets like Michael Madhusudan Dutt, Narayan Vaman Tilak and Vedanayaga Sastriar; educationalists like Krishna Mohun Banerjee, who is also the father of Bengali literature, and Principal S. K. Rudra; scholars like Professor Ramachandra the mathematician, whose work on the problems of maxima and minima and on differential and integral calculus made his name famous in the universities of Europe, Ram Chander Bose and L. D. Swamikannu Pillai; ministers of the Church like Lal Behari Dey, Nehemiah Goreh, Imam-ud-din, D.D., the most distinguished acquisition from Mohammedanism, Narayan Seshadri, who got his D.D. from McGill University of Montreal, W. T. Sathyanadhan and Bishop Azariah of Dornakal; publicists like Kali Charan Banerjee; mystics like Sadhu Sundar Singh; social servants like Pandita Ramabhai; women writers like Toru Dutt, Cor-

nelia Sorabji and Kamala Sathianathan; and public workers
like Dr. S. K. Datta and Mr. K. T. Paul—not to mention any
living person. These are men and women who would be
ornaments to any community and of whom any country would
be proud.

The Church in India has produced leadership of a very high
order and Indians have occupied with distinction places of the
highest responsibility. In many areas they have been placed in
administrative charge of mission districts formerly held by
European missionaries. Educational institutions with a long
succession of European principals have been handed over to
Indians. Indian Christian doctors have replaced Europeans in
several mission hospitals. There have been and are several
Indian moderators of Churches and Bishops of the Church of
South India and of the Church of India, Burma and
Ceylon, and the Methodist Episcopal Church. Wherever
Indians have been entrusted with such responsibilities they
are to a great extent proving themselves able, efficient and
trustworthy.

The Indian Church is also becoming more and more alive
to its responsibilities in the evangelization of India, as is evidenced by the number of indigenous missionary societies which
have been formed during the last fifty years. There are about
sixty of them now scattered all over the country, sponsored by
local churches and congregations and carrying on considerable
evangelistic work in the otherwise unoccupied areas of the
country. The earliest of them is the Indian Missionary Society
of Tinnevelly, organized in 1903, which now supports three
Indian missionaries in Dornakal in the Nizam's Dominions, at
a distance of over eight hundred miles from the home base, and
all their work, at a cost of Rs.48,000 per year. In 1905 the
National Missionary Society of India was organized at Serampore, with the object of uniting all Christian denominations into
one great society for the evangelization of India and adjacent
lands. It works with Indian men, Indian money and under
Indian management. Its work is carried on from fifteen centres
in nine provinces, at a cost of Rs.50,000 per year. Every live
church and parish runs or supports some form of indigenous

missionary work and uses voluntary lay men and women in its
evangelistic work.

The last and perhaps the greatest achievement of the Indian
Church is the great advance it has made towards the reunion of
the Churches. But this deserves a chapter to itself.

VIII

CHURCH REUNION

VERY early in the history of the missionary enterprise it was
realized that the perpetuation in the mission field of the several
denominations of the Christian Church in the west would
weaken the force of its witness and that care should be taken
to see that Christianity and not certain western forms of it was
spread. One of the speakers at the Missionary Conference in
Liverpool in 1860 raised the question and said, 'We ought to
carry to heathen countries Christianity as such, not English
Christianity. Our English forms of Christianity are to a large
extent the products of controversy. We ought carefully to
modify them before we settle them in other lands. We must
carefully look through our systems and get away from their
mere technicalities, their historical elements, their local peculi-
arities. The result will be a nobler exhibition of the oneness
of the Christian Church on the fields of heathenism than
Christendom has yet attained.' The speaker was obviously a
little in advance of his time, because the idea was criticized by
several other speakers, who put forward the well-known argu-
ment that every missionary 'honoured of God to be the means
of forming a Christian Church ought not to feel that he might
not give to that Church that form and complexion and general
order which he himself believed to be most for the edification
of the believer and the honour of Christ'; and the conference
itself did not record a positive minute on the question. There
was, however, no such hesitation in the missionary conferences
held in India even in those early days. From the very beginning it was accepted that the Church in India should not reflect

these divisions, but should present a united front to the forces against which it was fighting. Never in all the history of the Christian enterprise in India was it forgotten that the most effective witness to the power of Christ's gospel of love can come only from a united Church; and right through there have been attempts to bring about this unity, first in work and witness, then in comity and co-operation, and last of all in an organic union.

It was in the twentieth century, however, that active steps towards ultimate unity were taken. In 1901, a Federal Union took place between two Presbyterian Missions in South India —the United Free Church of Scotland Mission and the American Arcot Mission. In 1904 a similar Federal Union between the Congregational Churches of the American Madura Mission and Travancore London Mission was effected. In 1908, the South India United Church came into being by the blending of various Congregationalist and Presbyterian Communions. Having secured this union of non-episcopal ministries, the obvious next step was their union with communions possessing an episcopal ministry. It was, however, Bishop Whitehead of Madras who took the first effective step towards an organic union between the episcopal and non-episcopal Churches in South India by calling together for a conference, in 1910, the leaders of the Anglican Communion in India and of the South India United Church. It became evident, even in those early discussions, that the historic episcopate—the fact of the episcopate, not involving the acceptance of any theory about its origin or any doctrinal interpretation of its significance—was likely to be universally acceptable as the form of government in the United Church and that any union should involve no Christian community in the necessity of disowning its past or of calling into question the validity of the orders of other churches, two principles which are among the bases of the Church of South India.

The actual negotiations for union must be said to have begun at a special conference of Indian ministers called together by Bishop Azariah and the Rev. V. Santiago. Appropriately enough it was in Tranquebar that this historic conference took

place. About fifty Indian ministers and two European missionaries met and discussed the matter. Each of the Churches represented at the conference was asked to get one of their ministers
to prepare a paper on the distinctive features of the organization, religious teaching and practice of his Church and the
features that ought to be its contribution to a United Church,
should one come into being. Four papers were therefore read
at the conference by a Wesleyan, a Lutheran, a S.I.U.C.
minister and an Anglican, and after the reading of each there
was a discussion, exploratory in nature with no findings or
decisions. But it was felt that the question of the union of
the Church had become a challenge which could no longer be
ignored, ' as we face together the Himalayan task of winning
India to Christ—one-fifth of the human race '. The conference
felt that the Churches in India had been weakened by the un-
happy divisions imposed from without. It was convinced that
union was the will of God and was the teaching of the Scriptures. It therefore issued a manifesto and called upon the
Churches in South India to take up the matter in all earnestness.

The S.I.U.C. and the Anglican Church accordingly took it
up. The S.I.U.C. Assembly of 1919 agreed to negotiate for
union on condition that the resultant Church would be an
autonomous independent Church, and asked for a joint committee to begin negotiations. The Episcopal Synod of the
Church of England in India met in February 1920, and decided
to accept the invitation of the S.I.U.C. and appointed representatives to the joint committee, the first meeting of which
was held in March 1920. The appeal for union made by the
Lambeth Conference of July 1920 had far-reaching effects, but
the hope expressed that those ministers who had not received
episcopal ordination would accept a commission through such
ordination created unnecessary difficulties when negotiations
in South India had just been begun, and prevented further
progress for some time.

In response to an appeal to the other Churches in South
India to participate in the union negotiations, the provincial
synod of the Wesleyan Methodist Church of 1925 appointed

representatives to the joint committee. The coming of the
Methodists into the union negotiations was not only welcome,
but a great advantage in that they brought in a new element of
spiritual vigour and enthusiasm, and an overwhelming sense of
divine leadership. 'Being a Church with a tradition of authority, with very strict rules in regard to the reception and
training of ordinands and yet acknowledging the place of
prophetic inspiration and individual freedom, it was able to
form a bridge between the Catholic and Evangelical elements
in the Anglican and S.I.U.C. Churches.' The acceptance in
1928 of the position that the existing ministers of the three
Churches will be accepted as ministers of the Word and Sacraments in the Church after union was a great step in advance.
It was on this basis and as the result of 10 years' work that the
first 'scheme of union' was produced in 1929 by the Committee which excited great interest as the first attempt to unite
episcopal and non-episcopal Churches. The scheme was discussed by the Methodist South India Provincial Synod, the
General Council of the Church of India, Burma and Ceylon
and the General Assembly of the S.I.U.C., each of whom,
while giving general approval to the scheme, suggested modi-
fications for the consideration of the committee.

It is unnecessary to attempt to summarize the whole history
of the subsequent negotiations which went on for another
fifteen years before a formula acceptable to each of the negotiating Churches was found. The joint committee met every year
and tackled the stupendous problem with patience and un-
wavering faith, impelled by an overwhelming sense of God's
guidance and fully convinced that, inasmuch as union was
undoubtedly God's will and command, nothing should be left
undone to bring it about. The scheme, or portions of it, were
revised more than once. It was the Methodists who first decided
in 1943 to unite. The C.I.B.C. next decided in 1945 to join
and last of all, in 1946, the S.I.U.C. Further discussions clari-
fied the position to all concerned and in these last two or three
years the guidance of the Holy Spirit was clearly visible in
increasing co-operation and goodwill. In December 1946, the
joint committee decided that the time had come to inaugurate

the union and consider practical details such as the inauguration and consecration services, the dioceses of the United Church and the financial arrangements for Bishops and their selection. It met again for the last time in June 1947 and decided that the new Church be inaugurated on September the 23rd, 1947, at St. George's Cathedral, Madras.

The inauguration of the Church of South India which took place on that day was an historic and momentous occasion. A huge and unprecedentedly large congregation was present in St. George's Cathedral, Madras, and took part in the service in a spirit of high enthusiasm and great joy. There was an overwhelming sense of peace and gladness, of awe and worship. For twenty-eight years they and the people of God all the world over had been eagerly looking forward to this consummation. It was with hearts filled with gratitude to God and with a feeling of profound satisfaction that they took part. No one present at that service and at the consecration of the Bishops of the new Church which followed had the slightest doubt but that this was the work of the Holy Spirit, that we had been led by God Himself to such a consummation and that He was indeed present in the plenitude of His power amid His people. It was a repetition of what had happened several times in the history of the Christian Church down the ages—a special stirring up of people's hearts and a fresh outpouring of His Spirit for a special purpose.

The present writer was among those privileged to be present on this historic occasion. How thrilled we were when we heard the presiding Bishop say, ' In obedience to the Lord Jesus Christ, the Head of the Church and by the authority of the governing bodies of the uniting Churches, I do hereby declare that these three Churches are become one Church of South India.' The thrill and the spiritual exaltation of it are an unforgettable memory. Then came an overwhelming sense of privilege and responsibility that the great and unique chance of making this venture of faith should have been given to us, Christians of South India; and we prayed, laity as well as clergy, in all sincerity, truth and self-oblation, that God's Holy Spirit might continue to guide us as unmistakably as He had guided us in the past, and by His love might so enlarge our hearts that we whom He had been pleased to unite as brethren and to whom He had given a common task, might be ambassadors on behalf of Christ and ministers of the word of reconciliation for the bringing of the nations into His Kingdom. For it is obvious that this consummation of the union between the three Churches in South India is but a beginning; and that it will mean little to the Christian Church and the world if it does not lead us into ever-widening spheres of unity and concord. It is our prayer that we should continue to be open to the same guidance which led us into this adventure for God and our hope is that He in His own good time would use us for a wonderful manifestation of Christian brotherhood in the Church and would show us the way till the whole Church, His body, is one in form as in spirit as He wants it to be. We believe that it is within God's will and power that even greater miracles than this should happen in the Church, if not within the lifetime of this generation still in the fulness of time.

All persons who, at the time of the union, were communicant members of any of the uniting Churches became members of the united Church and were at liberty to receive communion in any of its churches. On the basis of the 1941 census, the Dornakal, Madras, Tinnevelly and Travancore dioceses of the C.I.B.C. brought into this Church a Christian community 499,966 strong, of whom 158,518 were communicants. The Hyderabad, Mysore, Madras and Trichinopoly districts of the Methodist Church brought 224,656 Christians, of whom 39,700 were communicants. And the Madras, North Tamil, Travancore, Madura, Kanarese, Jaffna, Telugu and Malabar councils of the S.I.U.C. contributed 292,562 members, of whom 65,462 were communicants. The total membership of the Church should now be about eleven lakhs.

The United Church has been formed not by the absorption of one by another, but by the comprehension of all valuable elements in the traditions of the uniting Churches, because they recognize that God has bestowed His grace with undistinguishing regard through all their ministries, which are therefore real ministries of the Word and Sacraments and will be accepted in the new Church without distinction or difference. It will also conserve all that is of spiritual value in its Indian heritage and will seek to express under Indian conditions and Indian forms the spirit, the thought and the life of the Church Universal. It is a comprehensive, indigenous and autonomous Church. In the matter of order and organization it is an episcopal Church, but not therefore an exclusive or sacerdotal one. It maintains that in every communion the true celebrant is Christ alone, who continues in the Church to-day that which He began in the upper room, and that in all ordinations and consecrations the true ordainer and consecrator is God who commissions and empowers His ministers.

The new Church is a unique achievement. It is an episcopal Church into which earlier episcopal and non-episcopal traditions have merged, for the first time in the history of Christendom. It is not the result of a hurried decision into which poor deluded lay folk or unwary clergymen of different denominations were hustled by interested parties. Nor is it a hastily conceived scheme prematurely brought into effect. It is the result of prolonged deliberations. Decisions were not man-made, but were impelled by an undeniable divine guidance which it would have been sinful to disregard.

It was not brought about by foreigners. The joint committee which carried out the negotiations and the Church councils which finally accepted the scheme and agreed to unite were overwhelmingly Indian in composition. One is prepared to go a step further and say that the final consummation was due to Indian leadership and Indian wisdom. We know how in other countries similar negotiations have not yet fructified. This new Church in South India is going to be a model for the Churches and denominations in other countries to follow—including the home Churches. It has so pleased God. It is not our doing.

However, we have not yet become one. We are not yet one Church except constitutionally. Real integration is yet to come. But it is coming. We are growing—some say rapidly, some say too slowly—into unity. All are agreed that we shall be one in a very real sense soon. The temporary compromises that have had to be made in order to make this growing together possible are well known. They are necessary and even proper, and do not detract from the value of the union. But we are not going to be uniform. Variety is going to be maintained. We are and shall be one Church, but there will be varieties of church life and practice within it, which will add to its richness. The result will be not a monochrome, but a mosaic.

The new Church is not a consummation, but just a beginning. It is not an achievement, it is an inauguration. It was never intended to be anything but a beginning. The whole scheme has been conceived and has been brought into effect in order that it may lead to a fuller unity, and leave the door open for other denominations to come in. It is hoped that in God's good time, every Protestant denomination in India will come into the new Church, and that the negotiations in North India will soon fructify and make possible a common united Church of India. There is a clear understanding that the Church of South India will endeavour to promote a similar union in the North, and on the conclusion of such a union will seek itself to be united to the Northern Church in an All-India United Church.

This new Church is intended to make possible a new type of creative Indian Christian life. It has given Indian Christians a free atmosphere to breathe in, in which they will be more at home, in which they will find an opportunity and an inspiration to bring their peculiar talents and their national genius to the feet of Christ. We Indian Christians have too long been mere copyists. We have not been creative enough. We have been cramped by circumstances so far. Now, freed from that bondage, with a Church of our own, we can bring into it all our gifts. So far, we have not created a Christian Indian theology, a Christian Indian art, a Christian Indian music, and a Christian Indian architecture; we have not produced distinctively Indian Christian devotional and theological literature. In the exultation of the new freedom from inhibiting traditions into which this Church has led us we must begin to think, to sing, to paint, to build, to preach, to adore, to worship, to witness, in a new creative way. A new generation is growing up in a new atmosphere, and it will, in God's good time and with His blessing, produce results which will redound to God's glory and to the good of the Church Universal.

IX

FAILURES OF THE INDIAN CHURCH

IT is easier to speak of the failures of the Indian Church than of its achievements, to point out aspects in the life of the new community where it fell short of the standards set by the new religion and handicapped its witness to the power and grace of the new faith. Most times it was in spite of the best efforts of the missionaries, though occasionally it was due partly to the missionaries who failed to give a correct lead to their flock.

The most obvious of these failures is the fact that even among Christian Indians caste has not yet, after two hundred years, been eradicated. Next to false doctrine, this is the most serious evil in the Indian Church, being the negation of the basic principle of Christianity, love. This is because in a few areas and especially among Roman Catholics, caste was for a long time tolerated in some form because it was difficult to ensure its complete removal. Christians in India, especially in the South, have not yet been convinced of the absurdity and evil of this horrid custom.

The Tamil Churches at their commencement contained a large element of nominal Christianity, from the fact that slaves and others, with poor knowledge and no character were baptized as Christians. Caste rules and customs were being observed by them among themselves though they might wish to conceal them or explain away their real force.[1] Caste is a relic of heathenism which the new Christians loved to retain.

It existed in the Indian Christian community in the retention

[1] *Missions in South India*, Joseph Mullen, (London, 1854.) p. 86.

of epithets indicative of caste, in the use of caste-titles after names, in unwillingness to live among those who did not belong to their own fraternity, in scrupulously avoiding meals in the houses of those belonging to a caste lower than their own, however clean and respectable in their habits, in refusing to inter-marry with other classes even when there was the necessary suitability. In its worst forms, it exhibited itself in a refusal to sit together in one church, in not sending children to schools attended by untouchable children, in *sudra* laymen refusing to attend services conducted by a low-caste priest, and in partaking of the Lord's supper before the lower-caste people received it. It was a fearful perversion of the spirit of the Gospel and a terrible caricature of the Christian faith. Thank God that its worst manifestations have now vanished: but the evil still exists in insidious forms within the Christian community.

Not that the evil was not recognized. It was agreed by both missionaries and Indian Christians to be un-Christian to retain caste titles and status after accepting Christianity. Indians had not become sufficiently Christian to shed the false pride which made them boast of their original caste status, and which prevented their full intercourse with their brethren of more lowly origin. And simply because to attempt to exterminate caste inside the Church was too much trouble and might have led to a few secessions some missionaries made the fatal mistake of permitting it while others tolerated it. Theoretically, the practice was admitted by everyone to be unbecoming, and yet the evil has persisted right down to the present day.

Apart from being theoretically un-Christian, this practice has led to several evil results. It has tended to keep the Indian Christian community divided into social sections, between which there is no inter-marriage, even though, at the present time, there is no one who is so foolish as to refuse to visit or to sit down and eat with another Christian. At times of competition, as for example when elections to church committees and church offices are held or when Christians as a community have to elect their representatives to the state legislatures and other public bodies, rival candidates who belong to different castes are set up and the whole matter is tainted with this un-Christian attitude.

It may surprise many to hear that even now, when posting pastors and catechists to villages and towns, the committees or individuals responsible for making such postings have to take into consideration whether the candidate will be acceptable to the people because of his origin. It is undoubtedly a most ridiculous position and should not be tolerated any longer. The authorities of the Church in India should be prepared to face any possibilities and refuse to bring such un-Christian considerations to bear on their decisions.

The second great evil which crept into the native Church very early was intemperance. Indians on the whole are a temperate people and drunkenness was not only very rare, but practically confined to the lower classes; even among them drinking was considered a vice. But when the British Government, with the intention of making revenue from drink, introduced the system of licensing liquor shops in towns and in villages and made the terrible mistake of renting out to middle-men the right to produce or distil country liquor and to establish shops for its sale, they made drink available to everyone, even in remote villages, and thus offered a temptation to poor people which many were unable to resist. The result was that there was a large increase in the habit of drinking spirituous liquors. Instances where whole families were wrecked because their male members wasted all their small earnings on it were becoming more and more numerous. Among the educated classes it became the custom to drink foreign liquor. It became fashionable to drink and to offer in one's home drink to one's friends in imitation of the Europeans in the country. As was pointed out by the Rev. Dr. Scudder of Vellore at the South Indian Missionary Conference, 1879, 'There has been in this respect a marvellous change in the country during the twenty-five years of my missionary experience. At the time of my arrival, intemperance was almost unknown in the rural districts, at least among the higher classes of the population. But now the spectacle of intoxicated Hindus, Brahmins not exempted, is no exceptional occurrence even in secluded parts of the country.

And sadder yet is the unquestionable fact of the rapidly increasing prevalence of the vice among the native Christians everywhere. It has already proved itself a malignant ulcer eating into the vitals of the native Church.'

The evil persisted in the native Christian community right down to the other day, when prohibition was introduced into the country by the new Government. No community has greater reason to welcome prohibition than the Christian community, because now it will be possible to eradicate this evil.

The third great defect is the failure on the part of both missionaries and Indian Christians to naturalize Christianity in the country, their failure to learn anything from Hindu philosophy and to evolve an Indian Christian theology in which both the strands of the Indian Christian heritage are woven into a new pattern acceptable to the Indian mind. The fact is that after two hundred years of Christianity the Christian message is still being presented in language unintelligible for the most part to the people of the country. For two centuries and more we have been studying Christian theology as presented by western minds and in western books and we have trained ourselves to think only along those lines. Indian Christians have not yet begun to think for themselves and to re-think the basic Christian conceptions in the light of the philosophical thought of their own country. The need for re-defining the Christian message in thought forms and in language that our countrymen will understand is now being fully realized. Opinion is, of course, divided as to whether Hindu philosophical thought can be used at all for the exposition of Christian belief. There is one school which thinks that the basic Hindu and Christian concepts are incompatible with one another and that therefore Hindu philosophy can give no real help in the interpretation of Christian doctrine. It must be admitted that certain basic ideas of Hindu philosophy are totally unacceptable even as a background for Christian thinking, as, for example, the doctrines of Karma and of rebirth. Yet it cannot be that the results of long centuries of thinking in India are totally valueless for Christian purposes. Some of the processes at least must be valuable and could be used in the elucidation of abstruse doctrines of Christianity. There must also surely be ideas embedded in Indian religious literature which can with advantage be used by Christian thinkers in the propagation of their religion in this country. But it is a fact that up till very recent times the need for exploring the possibilities of Indian philosophical thought in the evolution of a distinctly Indian Christian theology was not perceived and considerable harm has been done in this way.

The failure to increase social intercourse between Europeans and Indians must also be laid at the door of the Indian Christian community. With the presence of European missionaries in their midst, Indian Christians had and have a unique opportunity to bring about closer and more pleasant relationships between Westerners and Indians. On the other hand, even within the Christian community the distances that separated the missionary from the Indian has been one of the hindrances to the spread of the Christian gospel. Consciously or unconsciously missionaries from the west have kept themselves socially aloof from their converts and have, knowingly or otherwise, assumed an attitude of superiority which precluded any possibility of their moving on equal terms with them. This was perhaps inevitable in the early days, but was certainly inexcusable when Indian Christians rose in cultural and intellectual level. To refuse to mix with them socially was not a little due to snobbishness. Social customs and widely different eating and living habits justify it to a certain extent, but the unconscious influence of the ruling race to which the missionaries belonged had more to do with it than they realized, and so we had the spectacle of Christian missionary labour being carried on across a gaping social chasm. The Christian influence of the missionary on Indians would have been far greater had they been able to draw nearer to them.

This again is not an unrecognized evil which no serious attempts were ever made to remedy. The recent political and other changes in the country and the rapid advancement of at least a portion of the Christian community have brought about a much needed change in the respective positions of the missionary and his Indian Christian colleague and the other members of the community. Social relationships between Indians and Europeans have now, since India became independent, become more pleasant than at any time before and the same improvement has taken place within the Indian Church also.

But what is really to be deplored is the fact that, because of this difference in status and the lack of social equality even within the Christian group, it was not possible for the Christian community to bring about contacts between Europeans and Indians outside the Church. One of the factors which led to the growing estrangement between Indians and their British rulers which culminated in the 'quit India' demand was this lack of understanding and the failure to form friendships between Europeans and Indians. It is true that differences in social customs and usages which could not be got over by any amount of adjustment on the part of the two communities are mainly responsible for this unbridged gulf, but even so, as between professed followers of a religion of love, practising universal brotherhood, it should have been possible for the European and the Indian inside the Christian Church to have come closer together, had the European missionary not thought so much of his superiority in education and culture and the Indian Christian not been so obsessed with an inferiority complex. However, the root causes have been removed and a clearer demonstration of Christian brotherhood should follow.

Another thing which has hindered the cause of Christianity in the country has been the fact that Indian Christians have always stood aloof from the rest of the people as a distinct community and have segregated themselves socially and intellectually. The Indian Christian has always been regarded with considerable justification as 'a stranger in his own land and an alien to his own culture'. Such aloofness was not only natural and intelligible, but was perhaps also necessary during the early stages of spiritual evolution. It was then essential to absorb as much as possible of the cultural background of the new faith in order to feel at home in new and strange thought-forms and concepts accepted for spiritual reasons. The mistake lay in a certain indiscriminate over-enthusiasm for that culture and in avoiding altogether the indigenous culture of the people among whom the Christian had to live and who would be influenced by his life, his words and conduct. He acted and behaved as if Indian modes of life and Indian contacts would tarnish the purity of his spiritual life, and lived in India as though his spiritual home was in the west. This, it must be said, has to a large extent been changed. The Indian Christian no longer feels that to be faithful to his cultural heritage necessarily means disloyalty to Christ. But the original mistake has helped to segregate Indian Christians as a community and to make other communities think that Indian Christians were lost to the country in its political and intellectual progress.

The next great defect to be pointed out is that the Indian Christian community is still intellectually and even morally in its infancy. It has not yet attained maturity or become creative. It is true that there have been outstanding personalities in the community whose contribution in the field of thought, action and religion have been outstanding. Yet, even after making allowances for such, it must be admitted that the volume of its creative activity has been very slight. The failure of the Indian community to use its Indian philosophical heritage has already been pointed out. What is even more serious is that there has been so far no indigenous spiritual movement within the community. The gifts and graces of the Holy Spirit which are available in abundance to all believers and which should be utilized to create spiritual results have not been used. It is well known that adult converts from Hinduism who retain not merely memories but actual live contacts with their social and religious background are able to make a far more valuable contribution to the life of the new community than the Christians of the second, third and fourth generations. These latter are not only unable to make such contributions, but do not seem even to feel the need for such live contacts with non-Christians. These later generations of Christians have no inside knowledge of Hindu culture and are unable to see anything valuable in it to be utilized for the enrichment of the Church.

Another great failure on the part of the Indian Christian community is that in the main it has not yet learnt the importance of Christian giving and of the Christian stewardship of money. It is true that large sections of the Indian Church have become self-supporting and that some money is also being found for the support of missionaries to other places and for the support of Christian institutions. But the community as a whole has not realized its responsibility in the matter of making contributions for institutional work and the need for more sacrificial giving. It seems unlikely that for a very long time to come the Indian Church will be able to support the educational, medical and other institutions which it is gradually taking over from missions. What is indeed worse is that this prospect is not being viewed with embarrassment but with equanimity. It seems unfair to lay the blame for our un-Christian niggardliness for the support of the Church, her ministry and her institutions, on our missionary mentors, but the fact remains that our parsimoniousness is due as much to bad training and false thinking as to our own economic backwardness.

The next great defect is that the Indian Church is not sufficiently evangelistic. It is true that in recent times there have come into existence several indigenous missionary societies in the country which, relying purely on the support of the Indian Christian community, are carrying on missionary work in different parts of India and even outside. But, apart from the financial support, still very inadequate, given to such missionary societies, Indian Christians have not yet realized that it is personal evangelism and personal witnessing by Christian living that can win people over to Christianity. 'Every baptized Christian a missionary' was the slogan which Bishop Azariah inculcated in the mind of his flock. But this cannot be said to be true of the vast majority of our churches. Even to-day active evangelistic work is being carried on mainly under the auspices of missions rather than by the Church itself. The two great needs of the Indian Church at the present time are that the people should feel their responsibility for the evangelization of their country and for giving liberally and sacrificially for the support of God's work.

Lastly, it must be pointed out, without being considered to be unduly pessimistic, ultra-critical or purposely exaggerating, that, except in certain limited areas where spiritual leadership has been exceptionally strong, Indian Christianity has lost its original freshness and zeal, and especially in areas where Christianity has been established long enough to become merely traditional and physically inherited the story of Indian Christianity is one of increasing degeneration in spirituality, though of progressive advancement in economic and cultural life.

One of the most sincere friends of the Indian Church, Bishop Stephen Neill, has described the progress of Indian Christianity like this: 'Our old friend the village farmer is called plain Muthu. His son is Gnanamuthu, a trained teacher and a likely candidate for the ministry. His son has just joined the mission college and if he is sober and diligent he may go on until he blossoms out as Mr. John Gnanamuthu, B.A., B.L., Vakil of the High Court, and keeps a motor-car. *His* son will probably go to Cambridge and become a tennis blue.' This is a perfectly correct description of our outward progress during the last four or five generations. But there is absolutely no doubt, even though the good Bishop has not pointed it out, that this Cambridge blue, John Hoskyns Gnanamuthu, Esq., as he might call himself, J. H. G. Muthu for short, is spiritually a weakling compared with his great-grandfather, the plain Muthu. Muthu's fervent spirituality and simple faith were plainly visible, as were all the upper portions of his body, bare from the waist upwards. But the Cambridge blue's faith is smothered by his blazer with the college crest, and the flickering flame of his spirituality has long ago been extinguished by the cold of an English University education and by a deluge of intellectual irrelevancies. From a worldly point of view we of the present generation are far better off than were our grandfathers and great-grandfathers, but from the spiritual point of view it must be admitted that Indian Christianity has lost all round. It should now be the endeavour of everyone interested in the Indian Church to help us to recapture the simple faith, the fervent spirituality, the plainly visible power and the apostolic passion for souls which characterized the lives of our forefathers in what may well be called the apostolic age of Indian Christianity.

X

THE CHURCH IN THE NEW INDIA

On the fifteenth of August 1947, India turned over a new page in her long history, and started on a new era more glorious than all those that had gone before. As the Prime Minister, Sri Jawaharlal Nehru, said on that eventful day, 'The appointed day has come—the day appointed by destiny; and India stands forth again, after a long slumber and struggle, awake, vital, free and independent. The turning point is past. History begins anew for us, the history which we shall live and act and others will write about.' Nearly five years have passed since the country attained independence and we have also completed two years after becoming a Sovereign Republic. What is the condition of the country and the people to-day?

Everyone knew that the achievement of independence was not a consummation, but a beginning: that, after having achieved independence, we could not afford to sit back and enjoy its fruits, but that we would have to put our shoulders to the wheel, and work harder than ever to live up to our new-born status. It was admitted on all hands that it would be a very hard task and a tremendous responsibility. The Prime Minister told us, 'We have hard work ahead. There is no resting for any one of us till we make all the people of India what destiny intended them to be. We are citizens of a great country on the verge of a bold advance and we have to live up to that high standard. No nation can be great whose people are narrow in thought or in action.'

Our leaders fully realized the tremendous responsibility that had fallen on us and did all they could to impress it on us.

But what about us, the people? Have we shown 'a greater spirit of sacrifice and self-discipline than we showed in our struggle for freedom?' Have the rank and file shown any signs that they have understood even a little what this new independence means in terms of self-discipline and self-sacrifice? Let the leaders answer. 'The Government has had to face an uphill task. The co-operation of the people has been halting and even grudging. Whereas in self-governing countries every man identified himself with his nation and his government, here in India people do the contrary and each man wants to profit by self-government. How is Swaraj going to help me? Where and when can I advance my interests under Swaraj? These are the questions put to themselves by some of the political sufferers on one hand and a good fraction of the public on the other.' These are words which Dr. P. Sitaramayya, the then President of the Indian National Congress, wrote on the anniversary of Independence, 15th August 1949.

The result was that our leaders, while they could speak proudly of their achievements in and outside the country, when talking about the people, and their erst-while political followers, have had to be apologetic. 'Everyone also must realize that as a free citizen of independent India, he has to shoulder to some extent the burden of work and responsibility. Governments, however good they might be, can only function in a limited sphere. A democratic government requires even more the full co-operation and labour of the people in tackling any great problem. Criticism and self-criticism are always welcome, provided they do not take the place of work. To-day, India demands work from her children,' said Sri Jawaharlal Nehru, on the 15th of August 1949. He went on to talk about the problem of food and said that while the Government are tackling the problem, 'each man and woman can help in the production of food in some way or other and in avoiding waste. Let us therefore each one of us devote ourselves to the immediate work before us.'

But what is happening? The greatest challenge that is facing the nation at the present moment is that of hunger and scarcity of food. Millions of rupees are being spent in importing food, and yet the nation is worse fed than at any time before. More and more commodities are becoming scarce. The Grow More Food campaign inaugurated by the Government has been rendered almost a farce because the people do not co-operate.

What India is suffering from to-day is the lag between profession and practice, between ideals and reality; between first-rate leadership at the top and the dead weight of an ignorant, illiterate, apathetic and increasingly selfish mass of people who will not put themselves to any trouble for the common weal. There is visible deterioration in administrative standards. Corruption is rampant. Attempts made to put it down are half-hearted and ineffective. Herein lies the tragedy of the situation. While the top-ranking leaders of India have worked nobly to obtain for India a respectable and respected place among the nations of the world, internally there is deterioration in standards everywhere. What is going to save the situation is the determination on the part of the leaders to face and overcome difficulties. ' We are confronted with difficulties within and the horizon is overcast with dark clouds without. We have to gird up our loins and face them. God helps those who help themselves. Let us deserve God's help,' said Dr. Rajendra Prasad, the President of the Republic, on the eve of the first anniversary of the Republic. If the people heed this call and are wisely led by local leaders the situation will yet be saved.

The new India is a secular state. ' Secular ' is a word that has so far degenerated in modern speech as to connote frequently worldliness if not wickedness. Its use in this phrase will lift it once more to respectability. It was no doubt the abuse of religion which led to the secular conception of the state, but no disparagement of things spiritual is implied in the word. The preamble to our constitution makes this abundantly clear. ' We, the people of India, having solemnly resolved to constitute India into a Sovereign Democratic Republic and to secure to all its citizens Justice, social, economic and political, Liberty of thought, expression, belief, faith and worship, Equality of status and opportunity and to promote among them all Fraternity, assuring the dignity of the individual and the unity of the nation, do hereby adopt and give to ourselves this Constitution.' There is nothing sordid in such a conception of the state. There is no implication that the state will think of its duties and activities as merely mundane or that a purely scientific materialism is going to be the philosophy of the state, or that the things of the spirit are to be relegated to the background. The principles laid down in the new constitution are not inconsistent with the deeply religious strain which has been characteristic of the life of the Indian people. All that it means is that there is not going to be any state religion. This has been made quite clear by our leaders. The Prime Minister said in Parliament, 'This does not mean that religion ceases to be an important factor in the private life of the individual. It means that the state and religion are not tied together. It simply means the repetition of the cardinal doctrine of modern democratic practice, the separation of the state from religion, and the full protection of every religion.'

But at the same time the widespread expression of the national spirit which is current needs to be noticed. Contemporary nationalism in India is expressing itself in the revival of a culture which is predominantly Hindu in origin, and in a jealous pride in everything Indian. It is also expressing itself in a type of religious universalism to which the Christian can hardly subscribe. Religion is interpreted as a vague spiritual aspiration which does not demand an overwhelming loyalty to either certain principles or to a person. The similarity of all religions is emphasized. All living faiths are but different paths to the same goal, different ways up the mountain whose summit is the divine reality. The fundamental principles of ethics which are common to all religions are emphasized and there is the well-known confusion between religion and morality.

Lastly, new India is a country where Hinduism is renascent. It is a mistake to think that because of the Christian enterprise in the country Hinduism is shaking to its foundations and that its downfall may soon be expected. The progress of unbelief among the educated classes, the growing indifference of the

common people entitle us to conclude that it has been appreci-
ably weakened in its hold on the people, but it has still vast
numbers on its side, the prestige of hoary antiquity, the strength
of a great philosophy, the history of a persistent search after
truth by unnumbered sages and thinkers, and the unflagging
watchfulness of a powerful and hereditary priesthood, and the
whole fabric is strongly girded with the institution of caste
which raises almost insuperable barriers to any desire to aban-
don it. Hinduism has always shown resilience which has
helped it to revive even when severely wounded. This is what
two prominent leaders of Hindu thought say about it; and we
can accept what they say as true: ' After a long winter of some
centuries, we are to-day in one of the creative periods of
Hinduism. We are beginning to look upon our ancient faith
with fresh eyes. Leaders of Hindu thought and practice are
convinced that the times require, not a surrender of the basic
principles of Hinduism, but a restatement of them with special
reference to the need of a more complex and mobile social
order' (Prof. Radhakrishnan). 'During its long history of
more than forty centuries, Hinduism must have often presented
to an outsider the appearance of a religion in the last stage of
decrepitude. But somewhere in the interior of its amazingly
complex growth, there seem to be centres of vitality which
assert themselves again and again, and bring about a Renais-
sance, falsifying the predictions and perhaps the hopes of its
critics. To-day, Hinduism is passing through such a Renais-
sance' (Prof. D. S. Sarma).

Hindu society has adjusted itself to modern conditions. The
life and influence of Mahatma Gandhi has helped to quicken
the spirit of Hinduism more effectively than anyone else could
have done. So it is that we are faced not with an effete religious
system but with a resurgent Hinduism prepared better than
ever before, mainly because of the adjustments it has made in
modern times, to meet all onslaughts.

It is in this new India that the Church and the Christian
Indian community are now placed. Out of a total population
of four hundred and twenty millions, it forms two per cent or
one in fifty, while in that fifty there will be thirty-six Hindus,

twelve Muslims and one Sikh. There are still considerable tracts where Christianity has not penetrated, even after four hundred years of Christian work; certain strata in Indian society have been practically impervious to Christian influence.

Considering the matter further and taking only the non-Roman Christians, we find that, excluding some seventeen lakhs (a lakh is a hundred thousand) of children, there are eight lakhs of young people who have reached the age of decision and sixteen and a half lakhs of men and women, and nearly two and a half lakhs of older people. The striking force of Christianity in the country, if every one of these is taken to be a valiant soldier of the Cross, is only about twenty-five lakhs. The whole community has been gathered in by several different missionary societies and, except in South India where four denominations have united to form the Church of South India, is still divided between these different groups. The whole Protestant Christian community is scattered all over the country in 24,494 different congregations, each of which lives on an average in twenty-four different villages, from which it has to assemble for congregational worship. The number of ordained national workers is 3,198 and unordained national workers 11,323. There is one pastor for every eight congregations. How much real effective spiritual strength is possible if seventy-five Christians out of every hundred cannot read the Bible and cannot follow liturgical worship with a book, can only listen to the Scriptures and the prayers being read and cannot join in the singing, can well be imagined. Herein lies one of the greatest weaknesses of Indian Christianity—its illiteracy and therefore its incompetence, especially in villages where it should be ready to teach and to lead other communities in intellectual, social and spiritual matters. The Christian Church in India has had time enough to produce a hundred per cent literate community and its failure to do this is the most tragic failure of all.

It is this illiterate and ineffective community which now faces the new India, a Church still in its early adolescence, whose leaders are still mostly foreigners, a Church still largely dependent on outside help for man-power and finances, a Church whose rank and file have been recruited from the lowest of the low with but a small minority from the privileged classes or which has raised itself by means of education to a higher level, a Church whose relationship with the state is still to be defined in practical terms, a Church faced by powerful hostile forces but still inadequately equipped both spiritually and intellectually for the tremendous task which is facing it. But at the same time it is a Church which has taken root in the soil and has established itself. The Christian Indian community has by virtue of its educative activities and its service to the nation in the past won for itself an assured place in the national life from which it cannot easily be dislodged.

But the task which is facing the Church in this country is far more stupendous than any which ever faced any national Church in any other part of the world. It is, therefore, a critical time for the Church in India, when its strength and worth are going to be tested to the utmost. But new conditions also provide a new incentive to fulfil her divinely appointed mission, and offer a tremendous opportunity to serve the nation as it has a right to expect. Released from the handicap of its association with the political overlords, the Church in this country is now free to preach a Christ totally dissociated from the domination of the west. With the exit of the ruling race, Christianity will now be considered solely on its merits and will, therefore, receive a fairer deal than ever before. Christianity has never been faced with so doughty a foe as that which confronts it in this land. The ancient faiths of Greece and Rome which it overcame were infantile compared with the subtle wisdom and the mighty strength of modern Hinduism. The conditions of the conflict in India are entirely different. Its complex philosophical systems, the intellectual strength and influence of its religious leaders, the great inertia of the people, the mighty tyranny of caste, the all-embracing ritual of Hinduism, its severance of belief from conduct, its identification of religious loyalty with conformity to social order—all these constitute a more formidable combination than Christianity has ever previously faced.

The primary duty of the Church in India is, of course, to Christianize the country, not to proselytize, but to spread the good news of Christ, to be a witness for Him, all its members being participants in this endeavour. It is a new challenge to the Indian Church to deepen and strengthen her own spiritual life and to increase the spiritual effectiveness of her members. It will be the duty of the whole body of Christians in the country to present Christ to the people at large, not merely His religion and His message, but Christ Himself in all His beauty and attractiveness mirrored in their own lives. Christ is already accepted as an outstanding personality and as the type of perfect manhood, and His teachings are considered to be of the highest possible ethical standard. But he has not been accepted as divine or as the Saviour of mankind, having the supremest claim to man's loyalty. It is the foremost duty of Christians to prove this by the evidence of their own redeemed lives, a tremendous task, but a glorious opportunity.

In the second place, Christians should be ministers of reconciliation between the different communities. Such a ministry is sorely needed at the present time when communal distrust and ill-feeling are rampant. By the very fact that they are somewhat different in thought and habits from the rest of the people, they are in a better position to bring about better relationships between the different communities.

Thirdly, it is their duty to provide that spiritual undergirding to the life of the nation which seems to be the foremost necessity at the present time. At no time before was there in India such desperate need for men of Christ-like character. As one of the more literate and advanced sections of the nation, Indian Christians are making a valuable contribution to its intellectual life. But that is not enough. The distinctive and positive contribution of the Christian community in the land must be a spiritual one. They must help in the 'creation of the creators of a new society' in the country. They must unequivocally support the new order of things and co-operate unstintedly in all measures for the amelioration of the conditions of the people, but must be fearless critics when principles of justice and righteousness are contravened, must refuse to countenance those existing conditions which cannot be the will of God—slums, unemployment, low wages, glaring inequalities of opportunity, corruption, black-marketing and nepotism. The community should not ask (and has not so far asked) for privileges, concessions or leadership, except on the basis of acknowledged merit. The place from which Christians can render their most effective service is just that which other communities do not wish to occupy, where the 'drudgery and the chores of political work' have to be done. It is in the commonplace and the humdrum, in places where character is trained before it is exhibited, where people learn to work without any thought of reward, where they are content to work unseen, not asking for public recognition—it is in such places and positions that the Christian community can make its most valuable contribution to the national life, providing it with the moral power and the spiritual undergirding needed for its highest fulfilment.

Lastly, the Church in India must cease to be and to look foreign. Its leadership should gradually become more and more Indian. It must evolve a distinctively Indian type of administrative machinery, a new type of church life and organization modelled partially at least on ancient Indian forms. Its ministry must be changed so as to be less costly and more effective, making greater use of a spiritual call than of intellectual and theological training. At the same time it must evolve a type of scholar-thinker-priest whose business it will be to lead it towards a greater appreciation of Indian culture and philosophy and enable it to make an effective appeal to the intelligentsia. It must evolve a new theology as completely Christian as it will be distinctively Indian. It must work out new forms of worship, using all the resources of Indian art, architecture and music. It must adapt to Christian use indigenous methods of living and witnessing such as *ashrams* and *mutts*.

In this task the Church and the Christian community are protected by the safeguards which have been provided in the constitution of India, which not only secures for Christians their fundamental rights, along with all other citizens of the country, but also prescribes that 'the state shall not discriminate against any citizens on grounds only of religion' (among other things); and that all citizens are 'equally entitled to freedom of conscience and the right freely to profess, practise and propagate religion'; and that 'every religious denomination or any section thereof shall have the right to establish and maintain institutions for religious and charitable purposes'. Hence none of the Christian institutions in the country will be affected by the change in the political status of the country. The right to propagate religion thus secured by statute is no mean advantage.

Not only are Christians thus protected in the exercise and propagation of their religion, but the leaders of the nation, and everyone who counts for anything in public life, are wholly appreciative of the philanthropic, medical and educational work done under Christian auspices, though at the same time they look askance at all active evangelistic work calculated to convert the people to Christianity. They do not contemplate with equanimity any large increase in the number of Christians. As Mahatma Gandhi once said, 'Christian missions will render true service to India if they can confine their activities to humanitarian service without the ulterior motive of converting India or at least her unsophisticated villagers to Christianity.' It is, therefore, certain that while the Church and missions will be allowed to carry on their philanthropic activities, anything that savours of proselytism or leads to direct results such as conversion is likely to be looked upon with disfavour.

It is also obviously necessary that more and more of the Christian activity in the country should pass from mission auspices in Indian church leadership. There is a natural antipathy to anything that seems foreign-controlled. This does not, however, mean that we shall no longer need the assistance of the older Churches in personnel, funds and counsel. The Church in India will, for a long time to come, continue to need these and will be prepared to welcome as colleagues brethren in the faith from the older Churches. India is still the most glorious field for the operation of the evangelistic fervour of the Churches in the west. 'In the present world context, India may be God's laboratory. If the contemporary challenge to the Christian faith can be met in India, there is hope for all others.' But those who come out to serve her must come as servants, not masters, of the Indian Church, not as lords over

God's heritage, but as good shepherds, not as directors in the household of faith, but as helpers. India will need missionaries from the west, it would appear, for all time, and for a long time will need financial help. Let that be frankly stated. The Church in India cannot afford to dissociate herself from the Church in the west, and in the interests of Christianity should not be allowed to do so. The heritage and experience of the older Churches must always be made available to the Church in India as to all other younger Churches. Christianity is not a national religion, but a Catholic religion. No national Church, however gifted, should be allowed to cut itself off from the rest of Christendom. Much less can the young, inexperienced and so far comparatively ineffective Church in this country afford to isolate herself. The presence of the western missionary is invaluable and indispensable for the growth of the Church in this land. Besides demonstrating that Christianity transcends all national and racial bounds, it will be the means of ensuring the assistance of the western Church, both materially and spiritually. There are also certain specific contributions which missionaries from the west can make to our Christian life and work. We need them specially in our educational, medical and technical institutions. We need them in order to teach us certain virtues which we now lack, and in which they are strong. We need yet to achieve a higher sense of responsibility and learn to do our duty properly, even when there is no one to supervise our work. We need to learn to adopt a scientific attitude and acquire a spirit of detachment and objectivity in judging men and matters. We have yet to practise the exercise of impartial justice, to exhibit a readiness to accept loyally and work out whole-heartedly decisions that have been arrived at constitutionally. We have still not learnt to subordinate communal, linguistic and provincial prejudice to the corporate welfare of the Church and the glorification of her divine Lord. We have still to learn to appreciate and sympathize with the other man's point of view, and to attain to higher standards of integrity in personal and civic life. At the present time, when India is standing at the cross-roads of her destiny and is in sore need of men of character, and with the Christian striking force so small, so economically handi-capped and so meagrely equipped, mentally and spiritually, the Church and the Christian community in India need to be strengthened by all the support which the older Churches of the west can give. Christian charity demands it. Christian policy requires it. There is the need, and there will always be a welcome, in India for the consecrated man and woman who, impelled by the love of God in Jesus Christ, responds to the imperatives of the Gospel and comes out 'to minister and not to be ministered to'.

INDEX